Heinemann
Learning to Pass
Advanced ECDL AM3

Word processing

Using Word 2000

Advanced ECDL AM3

Word processing

Using Word 2000

Christine Blackham

www.heinemann.co.uk
✓ Free online support
✓ Useful weblinks
✓ 24 hour online ordering

01865 888058

Heinemann
Inspiring generations

Heinemann Educational Publishers
Halley Court, Jordan Hill, Oxford OX2 8EJ
Part of Harcourt Education Ltd

Heinemann is the registered trademark of Harcourt Education Limited

First published 2004

09 08 07 06 05 04
10 9 8 7 6 5 4 3 2 1

British Library Cataloguing in Publication Data is available
from the British Library on request.

ISBN 0 435 45582 6

Designed by Artistix, Thame, Oxon
Typeset by TechType, Abingdon, Oxon

Original illustrations © Harcourt Education, 2004

Cover design by Tony Richardson at the the Wooden Ark Ltd

Printed in the UK by Thomson Litho Ltd

Websites
Please note that the examples of websites suggested in this book were up to
date at the time of writing. It is essential for tutors to preview each site before
using it to ensure that the URL is still accurate and the content is appropriate.
We suggest that tutors bookmark useful sites and consider enabling students
to access them through the school or college intranet.

Tel: 01865 888058 www.heinemann.co.uk

Contents

CD-ROM

The accompanying CD-ROM contains:

Task files
Suggested answers.

Introduction

The Advanced ECDL Word Processing module is for those who have already completed the ECDL qualification or have intermediate word processing skills. You do not have to have studied or passed ECDL to take the stand-alone Advanced modules.

Unlike ECDL, which requires you to take modules that cover a selection of software packages, Advanced ECDL is more specialised; you study each module separately, and it is then tested and certificated separately. The Advanced qualification syllabus develops word processing skills that are not required for ECDL.

This book assumes that you have word processing skills at ECDL or Intermediate level and covers the additional skills that are required to enable you to achieve the Advanced ECDL word processing module. Included with the book is a CD that contains:

- the files you will need for the Tasks
- the answers to those Tasks.

The Tasks have been presented in a way that enables you to learn the skills in context with other skills, rather than as stand-alone exercises. These skills build up through the book with the more complex elements of the syllabus covered towards the end.

CD-ROM

To access the files on the CD-ROM:

1 Insert the CD into your CD-ROM drive.
2 The CD-ROM will run automatically.

Some machines may not support autorun and the CD-ROM will not start automatically. If this is the case:

1 Go to 'My Computer' and double-click on your CD-ROM drive.
2 The CD-ROM should now run automatically.

If it does not run, but instead displays a list of the files on the CD-ROM, then:

Double-click on the file default.htm. This will start the user interface screen

Note: If you are running the program from the CD-ROM, you must have the CD-ROM in the drive (including when you are trying to exit).

Getting started

Style conventions

Text in **bold** denotes Word menu or selection options.

To help you use the **Reference** file and the **Checklist**, the syllabus reference numbers (AM3 numbers) have been included at the end of each skill subheading, e.g. Use automatic text correction options (AM3.1.1.3).

PC setting conventions

Drop-down menus

It will be easier to follow the instructions if you set the drop-down menus on your machine to show all the options rather than the most recently used options.

Method

1 Right-click on the menu bar (underneath the blue bar at the top of the screen), select: **Customize**. The Customize dialogue box appears.

2 Click on the **Options** tab, then click in the tick box to deselect: **Menus show recently used command first**.

Handy Hint

If you are unsure which options are available to you as you work through the tasks, remember that right-clicking on an object will nearly always provide you with a drop-down menu of possibilities.

Toolbars

You may also want to see all the icons on the Standard Toolbar and Formatting Toolbar, rather than the shared row.

Method

To give each toolbar a separate row:

1 Use the method as above, but this time deselect: **Standard and formatting toolbars share one row**.

2 Click on: **Close**.

You should get three rows at the top of your screen, as shown in Figure 1.

Figure 1 Select a separate row for each toolbar.

Measurements

The instructions in this book and the assignment are in centimetres. If your machine is set to work in inches, use the following method to change your machine setting.

Method

1 On the main menu toolbar, click on: **Tools**, then select: **Options**.

2 In the Options dialogue box, select the **General** tab.

3 From the **Measurement units** drop-down menu, select: **Centimeters**.

Dialogue boxes

As you go through the tasks, you will be working with dialogue boxes. These boxes have blue bars across the top and most have a selection of tabs that contain various Word functions. For example, Figure 2 shows the dialogue box for the AutoCorrect function.

Figure 2 The AutoCorrect dialogue box

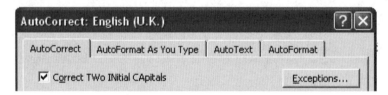

The functions displayed in a dialogue box are not appropriate to use all the time, but it is important that you become aware of what is behind the tabs.

Method

1 From the main menu bar, click on **Tools**, then select: **AutoCorrect**.

2 Click on the tabs to see the range of settings that you could apply to your document.

This book has been produced using Word 2000. You may be running different operating software, which makes the blue bar on the dialogue boxes look slightly different. For example, if you are running Windows 98 or Windows 2000 software in the background, i.e. your Operating System, the buttons on the blue bar at the top of the dialogue boxes have square corners and are black, rather than the more rounded white buttons as illustrated in Figure 2. However, the content of the dialogue boxes is exactly the same, whichever operating software you have on your PC.

Acknowledgements

The publishers would like to thank Duncan Grey, Project Gutenberg for permission to reproduce the Samuel Pepys diary extracts. The text can be seen at the Sanuel Pepys website at http://www.pepys.info and the whole of the text is also available from Project Gutenberg.

The Health and Safety (Fees) Regulations © Crown Copyright 1989.

Screen shots reprinted with permission from Microsoft Corporation.

Every effort has been made to contact copyright holders of material reproduced in this book. Any omissions will be rectified in subsequent printings if notice is given to the publishers.

In this task, you will cover the following skills:

- Select different viewing options.
- Creating multiple column layouts.
- Change column width and spacing.
- Apply different effects to text.
- Apply paragraph shading and borders.
- Use widow and orphan controls.
- Insert a watermark to a document.
- Apply text wrapping.
- Insert footnotes and endnotes.
- Create an index.
  - o Select text for the index.
  - o Create the index from the marked entries.
- Add password protection to a document.
- Print a selection of pages.

Scenario

You have been given a file that contains text from a Daniel Defoe book. The owners of the file have requested that you produce a document to be handed out at a meeting.

Unfortunately, the file was originally produced on a word processor that was not able to format, and what you have received is unformatted text. As this is a first meeting and the attendees are new to the group, the Chair of the meeting would like it updating. Your task is to transform the text into a document that will capture their attention.

1.1 | *Select different viewing options*

Method

1 In Word, **Open** the file **Text for Task 1** from the Task Files folder on the CD-ROM.

2 As you can see when you click on the **Print Preview** icon , the document is 8 pages.

3 **Save** your document as: **Task 1**.

4 You need to work with the document in **View**: **Print Layout** so that 'what you see is what you get'. There are three other views that could have appeared on your screen. Your document should look like Figure 1.1.

Figure 1.1 Opening a saved file in View: Print Layout

```
Tour Through the Eastern Counties of England - Daniel Defoe

I began my travels where I purpose to end them, viz., at the City of London, and
therefore my account of the city itself will come last, that is to say, at the latter
end of my southern progress; and as in the course of this journey I shall have many
occasions to call it a circuit, if not a circle, so I chose to give it the title of
circuits in the plural, because I do not pretend to have travelled it all in one
journey, but in many, and some of them many times over; the better to inform myself
```

You should be able to see the text in a line across the page and be able to see the outside edges of the 'paper', i.e. there is a grey background.

5 Try changing the view to look at the different options. Click on: **View** and then select in turn: **Normal**, **Web Layout**, **Print Layout** and **Outline**.

6 Leave your document in **Print Layout** view.

1.2 Creating multiple column layouts

The first formatting you are going to do is to put the document into newspaper columns, i.e. vertical columns of text so that the reader does not have to read across the full page width. You will set the text in two columns per page.

Method

Make sure that the I-beam cursor is on the page. Two methods are given below:

METHOD 1:

o Click on: **Format: Columns**, then select: **Two** (see Figure 1.2).

Figure 1.2 Selecting two text columns in Format: Columns

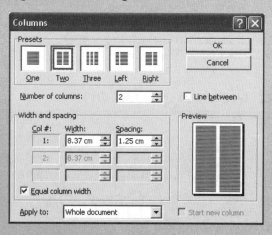

o Click on: **OK**. The document should now be in two columns.

METHOD 2:

o Click on the **Columns** icon on the Standard Toolbar.

Figure 1.3 Click on the Columns icon on the Standard Toolbar

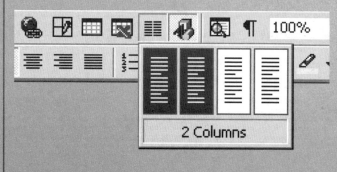

Practise this skill using both methods.

Set the document to three columns.

Now set the document to two columns with a wider left-hand column. To do this you need to use the first method to make the Columns dialogue box active.

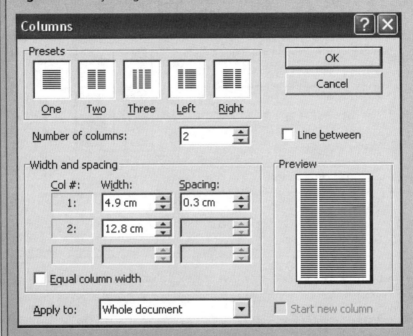
You should have two columns of text including the heading.

1.3 Change column width and spacing

It now looks as though the columns are too wide. You will modify this and put a line down the centre of the columns to separate them.

Method

1 Click on: **Format**: **Columns**.

2 Make the selections as shown in Figure 1.5. Look at the Preview box to check the changes.

Figure 1.5 Changing the column width and checking the changes in the Preview box

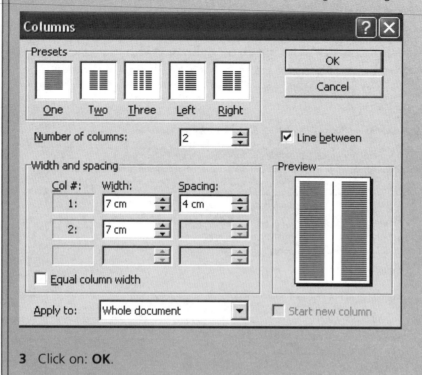

3 Click on: **OK**.

The text could be presented as newspaper columns with each line of text the same length.

Method

1 Hold down the **Ctrl** key and press: **A** to select all the text in the document.

2 Click on the **Justify Alignment** icon ▤.

3 Click anywhere on your document to remove the 'reverse video' effect caused by selecting all the text.

The title heading of the document is currently in the first column. It should run along the top of the page above the two columns.

Method

1 Select the heading text.

2 Select: **Format**: **Columns**: **One**.

3 Click on: **OK**.

Figure 1.6 Setting the heading text to one column

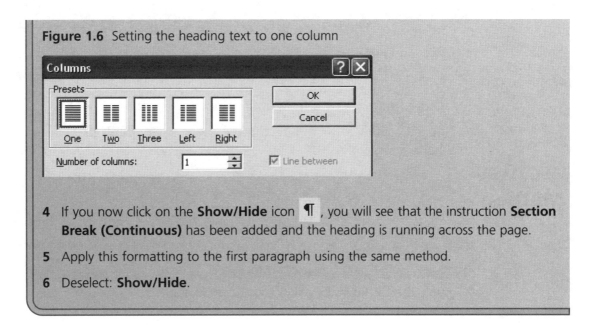

4 If you now click on the **Show/Hide** icon ¶ , you will see that the instruction **Section Break (Continuous)** has been added and the heading is running across the page.

5 Apply this formatting to the first paragraph using the same method.

6 Deselect: **Show/Hide**.

1.4 *Apply different effects to text*

You are going to change the font of the heading to Arial, 16 point, bold, with a shadow effect.

Method

1 Select the title text using the I-beam cursor or by triple-clicking.

2 Right-click (you must make this a quick click) to get the correct pop-up menu.

Handy Hint

If your right click is too slow, you will get the Move/Copy pop-up menu, which does not have the Font option.

Or:

3 Select **Format** from the main menu bar, then **Font**.

4 Make the following selections:

- o **Font:** Arial
- o **Size:** 16
- o **Font Style:** Bold
- o **Effects:** Shadow

Figure 1.7 Applying text effect options from the Font menu

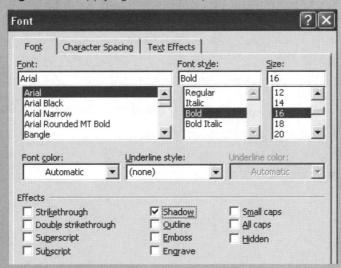

5 Look in the **Preview** box to see how your selections have affected the text.

6 Click on: **OK**.

Try more of the various Effects options, for example:

- Apply the Strikethrough effect to the second paragraph that starts with the words, 'I hope it will'.

Method
1 Select all the text in the paragraph either by triple-clicking or by using the I-beam cursor.
2 Select: **Format** from the main menu bar, then select: **Font: Strikethrough**.
3 Click on: **OK**.

- Apply the Superscript effect to the 'rd' in the date on the first line of the third paragraph.

Method
1 Select 'rd' after the number 3.
2 Select: **Format** from the main menu bar, then select: **Font: Superscript**.
3 Click on: **OK**.

- Apply a Subscript effect to 'Daniel Defoe' in the heading.

Method
1 Select 'Daniel Defoe'.
2 Select: **Format** from the main menu bar, then select: **Font: Subscript**.
3 Click on: **OK**.

- Try the Underline style drop-down menu on the heading. You can underline the words only and apply different styles, for example dotted, dashed or a combination of both. Do not add this effect to your work.

1.5 Apply paragraph shading and borders

You are now going to format the first paragraph with shading and a border.

Method
To apply the shading:
1 Triple-click in the first paragraph (or use the I-beam cursor to select the text).
2 Select: **Format** from the main menu bar, then select: **Borders and Shading**.
3 Click on the **Shading** tab, then select: **Gray-25%**. Apply to: **Paragraph**. Do not click on OK.

To apply a border around the paragraph:

1 Triple-click in the first paragraph (or use the I-beam cursor to select the text).

2 Select: **Format** from the main menu bar, then select: **Borders and Shading**.

3 Click on the **Borders** tab, then select:

   o **Setting**: Box
   o **Color:** Blue
   o **Width:** $2\frac{1}{4}$ pt

Take time when selecting the colour – hold the cursor still over the colour and you will get a pop-up text to confirm exactly which colour you are selecting.

4 Make sure that the **Apply to box** shows: **Paragraph**.

5 Click on: **OK**.

Figure 1.8 Applying a border around a paragraph

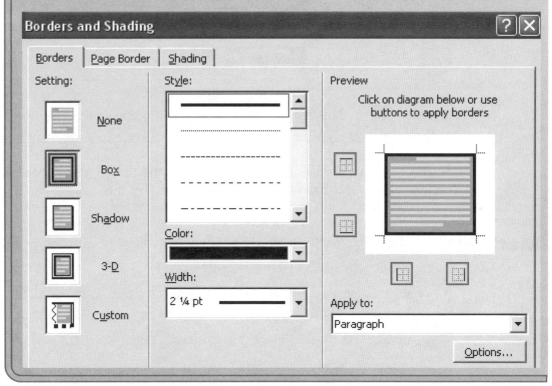

The same method can be used to apply a border to any amount of text. For example, to apply a border around the whole page you would select the **Page border** tab.

Your borders do not have to be straight lines: you can choose to have Art around the edges of your document.

Method

1 Click on: **Format** from the main menu bar, then select: **Borders and Shading**.

2 Click on the **Page Border** tab, then click on the drop-down **Art** menu. Look at the various options and make a selection. An example is shown in Figure 1.9.

Figure 1.9 Using the Art drop-down menu on the Page Border tab

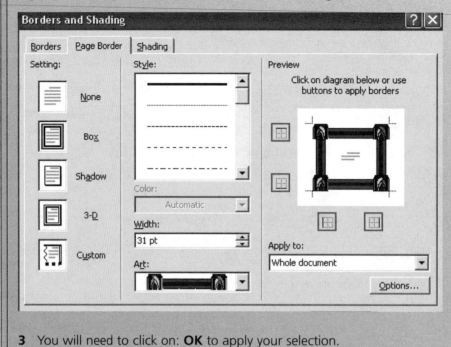

3 You will need to click on: **OK** to apply your selection.

Some of the Art borders flow over the top of the text. If you wanted to use these Art options, you would have to reformat your text. Try this:

Method

1 Select: **File** from the main menu toolbar.

2 Select: **Page Setup**.

3 Select the **Margins** tab and change the **Top**, **Bottom**, **Left** and **Right** margins, for example to 2.5 cm.

4 Apply to: **Whole document**, then click on: **OK**.

5 Click on the **Undo** icon to revert back.

As these Art borders are not appropriate for our purposes, make your final selection as follows.

Method

1 Click on: **Format** from the main menu bar, then select: **Borders and Shading**.

2 Click on the **Page Border** tab, then click on the drop-down **Art** menu.

3 Select the following options:

  ○ **Setting**: Box
  ○ **Color:** Green
  ○ **Width:** $\frac{3}{4}$ pt
  ○ **Apply to:** Whole document

Handy Hint

You have to select **Art**: **(none)**, before you can select a colour and width.

1.6 *Use Widow and orphan controls*

You will see when you scroll through your document that you have a line left on its own at the bottom of the column (orphan) or a line on its own at the top of a column (widow), i.e. it has become separated from the rest of the paragraph. To stop this happening you need to apply the widow and orphan control.

Method

1 Select all the text (**Ctrl +A**).

2 Click on: **Format** from the main menu bar, then select: **Paragraph**.

3 Select the **Line and Page Breaks** tab.

4 Select: **Widow/Orphan control**.

Figure 1.10 Selecting Widow/Orphan control in Format: Paragraph

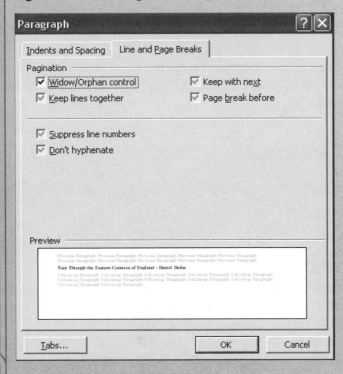

If you have grey ticks in the boxes (as in the illustration above) then some of the text has already been formatted. Click in the Widow/Orphan control tick box until you get a black tick indicating that all the selected text has the formatting applied.

5 Click on: **OK**.

Click down on your document and scroll through your document again. You should not see any 'lonely' text.

Insert a watermark

The literary group would like a watermark adding to the centre of the document to prevent it being photocopied and 'passed off' by anyone else.

Method

1 Select: **View**: **Header and Footer**.

2 Run the pointer tool over the icons in the pop-up dialogue box until you see **Show/Hide Document Text**.

3 Click on the **Show/Hide Document Text** icon

Figure 1.11 Selecting the Show/Hide Document Text icon

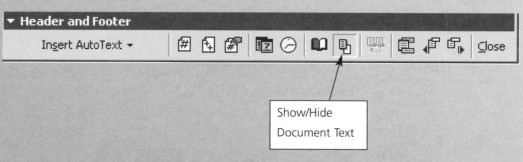

Show/Hide
Document Text

Don't panic! The text in the document will disappear so that you can work on inserting, for example, an image or a text box. For this document, you are going to insert an image from ClipArt.

Method

1 Select: **Insert**: **Picture**: **ClipArt**.

2 Select the **Pictures** tab. Choose an image that represents books. Depending on the software you have installed on your machine, you may find one in **Academic**.

3 Click on the **Insert clip** icon.

Figure 1.12 Inserting a picture from ClipArt

Insert clip

The image should now be in the header.

4 Close the **ClipArt** dialogue box by clicking on the 'X' in the top right-hand corner.

5 Click on your image to select it. This ensures that the **Picture Toolbar** is active. Click on the **Image Control** icon, then select **Watermark**. The image should now have changed to appear grey.

Figure 1.13 Selecting Watermark from the Image Control icon on the Picture Toolbar

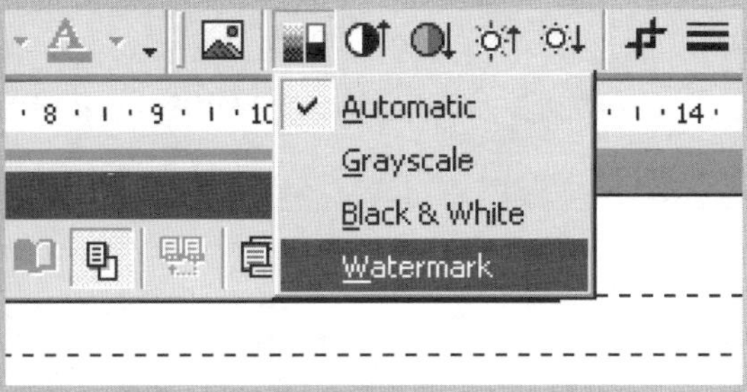

The image needs placing in the centre of the page: at the moment it is at the top of the page. You may find that the image you have chosen will not move when you click down (hold the mouse button down) and drag. This is because the image is formatted to be 'in line with text'. In this case, you will have to change the formatting of the image.

1.8 *Apply text wrapping*

Method

1 Double-click on the image to access **Format Picture**.

2 Select the **Layout** tab, then select: **Behind text**. This selection will allow the text to flow over the image and allow you to move the image.

Figure 1.14 Selecting Behind text to flow text over a chosen image

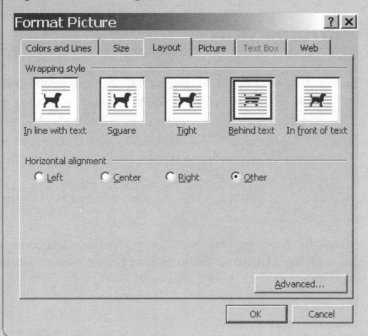

You can also centre the image vertically and horizontally using the Format Picture dialogue box, rather than making a 'best guess'.

Method

1 In the **Format Picture** dialogue box, click on the **Advanced** button (Figure 1.14).

2 Select the **Picture Position** tab.

3 Make the selections shown in Figure 1.15. You will need to click on the **Alignment** radio buttons (the small circles) before accessing the drop-down menus.

Figure 1.15 Centring an image vertically and horizontally in Format Picture

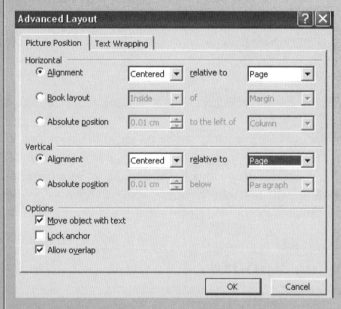

4 Click on: **OK** to clear the **Advanced Layout** dialogue box, then click on: **OK** to clear the Format Picture dialogue box. The image should now be in the centre of your page.

5 Click on: **Close** on the **Header and Footer** dialogue box. The image should move to the back of the text and appear on every page.

1.9 *Insert footnotes and endnotes*

The speaker for the evening would like notes adding to the document. Two footnotes need to be included and two endnotes. The footnotes will appear at the bottom of the relevant pages and the endnotes will appear in a list at the end of the document.

Endnotes

These are the two endnotes that are to be inserted into the document. The position of each endnote is given in brackets.

- **Maps are available on request** (position at the end of second paragraph).
- **Extra copies can be obtained from Reception** (position after the word 'England' in the title).

1 Click in the text at the appropriate point, i.e. at the end of the second paragraph after the words 'opportunity to see them' to insert the note reference marker.

2 Click on: **Insert** from the main menu toolbar. Select: **Footnote** – this will access the **Footnote and Endnote** dialogue box.

3 Select: **Endnote**. Leave the defaults as they are.

You can change the symbol if you wish, but you will have to remember to change it for subsequent endnotes.

4 Click on: **Options**, to access the **Note Options** dialogue box.

Figure 1.16 Inserting an endnote using the Note Options dialogue box in Footnote and Endnote

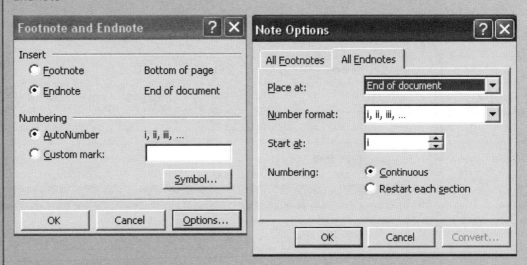

5 Click on the **All Endnotes** tab.

You could reposition the endnotes (or footnotes) and change the formatting at this point if you wished. For this task, we want the endnote to fit the options shown below.

6 Select the following endnote options (as illustrated in Figure 1.16).

- **Place at**: end of document
- **Numbering**: continuous
- **Number format**: set to Roman numerals.

7 Click on: **OK** to close the **Note Options** dialogue box, then click on: **OK** to close the **Footnote and Endnote** dialogue box.

8 The cursor will move to the end of the document. Key in the text you want to appear, i.e. **Maps are available on request**. If you now run the cursor over the position of the Endnote at the end of the second paragraph (use **Ctrl + Home** keys to get to the top of the document), you will see a symbol attached to the cursor and the Endnote text on- screen.

If you wish to delete the endnote (or footnote) for any reason, you do this by selecting the note reference marker in the main body of the document and pressing the Delete key.

Repeat this method for the second endnote, i.e. **Extra copies can be obtained from Reception**. You will notice that Word recognises that the second endnote you inserted should go before the first endnote.

Footnotes

These are the two footnotes that are going to be inserted and positioned at the bottom of the page. The exact position of each footnote is given in brackets:

- **of an ancient Roman Catholic family** (position after the name 'Fanshaw').
- **Mr Martin Creswell** (position after the word 'Newbrugh').

Method

To find the position quickly where the footnotes are to be inserted:

1 Click on: **Edit** from the main menu toolbar, then select: **Find**.

2 In the **Find what** box, key in the word 'Fanshaw'.

3 Click on: **Find Next**. The cursor moves directly to the word and highlights it.

4 Close the Find and Replace dialogue box by clicking on the '**X**' or the **Cancel** button.

Figure 1.17 Using the Find what box to access a position quickly

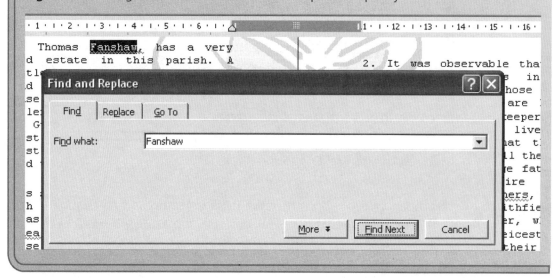

Method

To insert a footnote:

1 Position your cursor after the 'w' in Fanshaw and click.

2 Click on: **Insert** from the main menu toolbar, then select: **Footnote**.

3 Select: the **Footnote** radio button.

4 Click on: **OK**. The cursor will move to the bottom of the page.

5 Key in the text you want to appear.

Repeat this method for the second footnote.

Check that your footnotes and endnotes appear in the document by moving the pointer close to the Footnote/Endnote markers in the text.

1.10 Create an index

Part of the discussion on the Daniel Defoe document is going to focus on the geography of the area in the novel. Being able to focus quickly on certain geographical features will help the speaker to make his or her point. You can mark these items using an index.

Indexes are similar to producing a table of contents in that Word will automatically search and produce a list for you. You will see later that tables of contents are produced from text that has a specified style applied to it, whereas an index is defined by determining the exact words you want to appear in your index and hence the words you want Word to search for.

There are two parts to producing an index. The first part is to select (mark) the text; the second is to create the index from the marked entries.

Select text for the index

You should now have the Mark Index Entry dialogue box on-screen.

The next step is to mark the words you want to be indexed, i.e. 'rivers', 'canals', 'villages', 'marshes' and 'towns'. You may need to use Find and Replace if you cannot immediately see these words.

1 Find the word 'river' using **Edit**: **Find**. It does not matter if the word that you highlight is not the first occurrence of the word in the document.

2 Click in the **Main Index Entry** box. The word 'rivers' should appear in the box.

3 In page number format, select **Bold** and **Italic**. This determines the style in which the page numbers appear in the index.

4 Click on: **Mark All**. This tells Word that you want all instances of the word 'river' marking.

Have a look at your document now. Word has automatically turned on the Show/Hide facility. You should be able to see the 'XE' marker in brackets after the selected words.

Figure 1.18 Selecting index items using the Main Index Entry dialogue box and the Find and Replace dialogue box

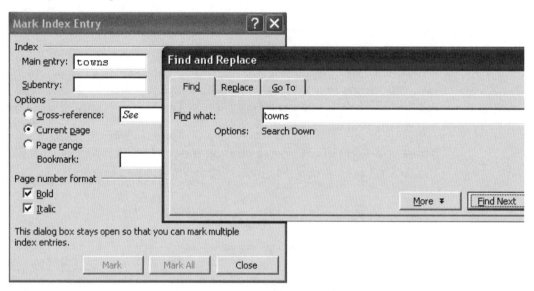

5 Click on your document. The Mark Index Entry box should remain on-screen so that you can continue to use it.

1 Find the word 'canals' using **Edit**: **Find**.

2 Click in the **Main Index Entry** box, and 'rivers' will change to 'canals'.

3 Click on: **Mark All**.

4 Repeat this sequence (steps 1 to 3), marking the words 'villages', 'marshes' and 'towns'.

5 Click on: **Close** to remove the Index and Tables dialogue box.

6 Click on: **Cancel** to close the Find and Replace dialogue box.

The first part of creating an index in Word is complete.

The second part, creating the index from the marked entries, is the easier part. The most important instruction to remember is that you must position the cursor at the point where you want the index to appear.

Create the index from the marked entries

You should now have an index positioned at the end of the text and before the endnotes. This is the default index. You can amend this by going back into Index and Tables and changing the options.

Figure 1.19 Setting the index style on the Index tab in Index and Tables

You can see easily from Figure 1.19 that 'canals' only appears once in the document, whereas 'towns' appears four times. [Note: Depending on how your PC is set up, your page numbers may be different.]

Add password protection to a document

As your work area is a shared area, you may want to be totally confident that your work will not be lost or modified. One way you can do this is to add a password to your document.

Method

With your document on-screen:

1 Click on: **File**: **Save As**.

2 Click on: **Tools**, then select: **General Options**.

Figure 1.20 Click on Tools, then select General Options

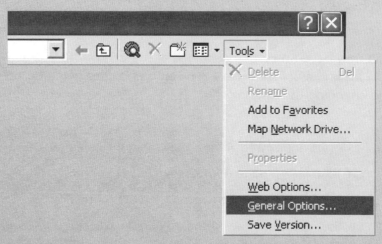

3 You can choose two passwords: one to open the document and one to modify the document. The second password will allow others to view the document but not to modify it.

Figure 1.21 Entering passwords to open and modify the document

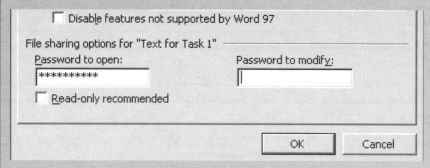

Handy Hint

CAUTION: Passwords appear as asterisks. Be very careful that you key in correctly and remember that passwords are case sensitive.

4 Key in your password.

5 Click on: **OK**. You will be asked to confirm the password to re-open the file.

6 Click on: **OK**.

7 Save your document as: **Task 1**.

8 To check that your password is working, close the document and re-open it.

1.12 Print a selection of pages

You will print the first and last page of your document to check style and layout.

Method

1 Click on: **File**: **Print**.

2 In **Page Range**, select the **Pages** radio button and key in: **1,9** (if 9 is your last page, otherwise key in your last page number).

3 In **Zoom**, select from the **Pages per sheet** drop-down menu: **2 pages**. Printing in this way will save time, paper and ink.

4 In **Printer**, check that the name of your printer is selected from the **Name** drop-down menu.

Figure 1.22 Selecting print options in File: Print

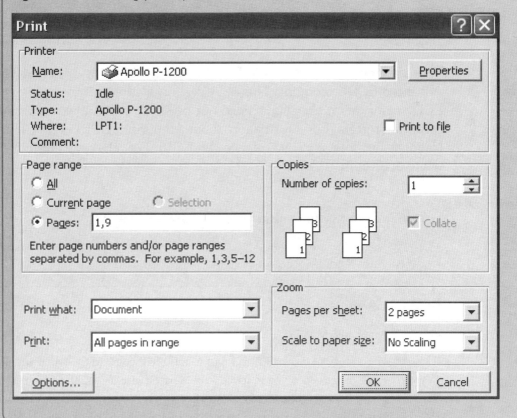

When selecting pages for printing:

- A comma is used to select individual pages. For example, if you wanted to print pages 1, 3 and 8, you would key in 1,3,8.
- A hyphen is used to indicate a range of pages. For example, if you wanted to print the first page and the last 3 pages of a 9-page document, you would key in 1,7-9.

Look at the following print options:

- The **Print what** drop-down menu allows you to select which element of your file you want to print, for example, Document properties.
- The **Print** drop-down box allows you to print all the pages (default). Alternatively, you can select to print odd number pages or even number pages only.

Handy Hint

In **Print**, the **Options** button allows you to format your printing output to your own requirement. **Draft output** and **Reverse print order** are two very useful selections:

- Draft output saves on ink.
- Reverse print order saves you having to re-order your pages after printing. However, the disadvantage of Reverse print order is that it can slow down the printing process.

Practice Task

Task 1

These exercises are included to help the candidate in his or her training for the Advanced ECDL program. The exercises included in this material are not Advanced ECDL certification tests and should not be construed in any way as Advanced ECDL certification tests. For information about Authorised ECDL Test Centres in different National Territories, please refer to the ECDL Foundation website at **www.ecdl.com**.

Open the File named **Madrid** from your Task Files folder.

The following text should appear. It is for a flyer that you have been asked to produce for a local travel agent's holiday to Madrid.

MADRID

Panoramic Madrid

The history of the majestic city of Madrid will come to life when you allow your guide to introduce you to its incredible past. Once an Arabian Fortress, this city is now a thriving cultural centre bursting with monuments, galleries and museums. You will even see Santiago Bernabeu Stadium, home of the famous Real Madrid football team.

Artistic Madrid

Introducing one of the world's greatest art galleries. The Prado Museum holds major works from all the great schools of European art, including paintings by Rubens, Rafael, Goya and El Greco. Let our guides take you there. Then move on to explore the 18th-century Royal Palace.

Toledo, El Escorial, Valley of the Fallen

Journey south of Madrid into a long forgotten world as you discover the ancient city of Toledo, once the medieval capital of Spain. Become familiar with the life of a monk as you tour El Escorial Monastery, and spare some thought for the dead of the Spanish Civil War in the Valley of the Fallen - the history of this country will simply amaze you.

Madrid by Night

At night, Spaniards put on their dancing shoes and step out for an evening of fun, feasting, and friendly flirting. After a panoramic drive to see the city lights, you'll join the locals at the Florida Park nightclub. Enjoy a fabulous tapas meal, a flamenco show, and all-night dancing.

1 Display the text in landscape with four columns of equal width.

2 Change the spacing between the columns to 2 cm.

3 Display the text fully justified.

4 Apply pagination, widow and orphan control.

5 Centre the heading 'MADRID' so that it appears above columns 2 and 3.

Handy Hint

Before you align the heading, highlight the word 'MADRID' and format to one column. This inserts a section break.

6 Place a 3 pt shadow border around each subheading. Apply to text.

Handy Hint

If the subheading is on two rows, you will need to apply the border to Paragraph, <u>not</u> Text.

7 Change the subheadings to Arial, bold, blue, 14 pt.

Handy Hint

If you need to reformat the borders, because the subheading has gone onto two lines, you will need to remove the border from the 'text'.

8 Change the heading to bold 48 pt.

9 Apply an outline effect to the heading.

10 Shade each subheading with yellow.

Handy Hint

If you have done this correctly, the yellow colour will not 'fill' the border but will flow outside the box.

11 Insert an appropriate image for a coach holiday from ClipArt and set the image as a watermark in the header.

Handy Hint

Key in 'bus' in the Search for Clips box.

12 Format the coach image so that text flows over the top and bottom. (AM3.1.1.6)

13 Resize the image so that the height is 7 cm.

14 Position the image at the bottom right-hand side of the page.

15 Ensure that you can see the watermark.

16 Expand the character spacing on the heading to 200%.

Handy Hint

Format: Font.

17 Insert an appropriate image from ClipArt that represents sunshine.

18 Position the image at the top of column 2, and resize if necessary. Apply a text wrap so that the text does not flow over the image.

Handy Hint

Apply the text wrap before you move the image.

19 Insert column breaks to ensure that each subheading starts at the top of the column.

Handy Hint

Position the cursor in front of the subheading and select: Insert: Break: Column Break: OK. If the image moves around, drag it back into position.

20 Adjust the size of the text in column 1 so that the text fills the column without pushing text out from the other columns.

21 Create the footnote 'See leaflet 6' after the word 'dancing' at the bottom of the fourth column. (AM3.3.3.1)

22 In Symbol, apply the heart as a Custom Mark.

23 Spell-check your work.

24 Print the current page only. (AM3.6.1.3)

25 Save your work as **Task 1 Answer**.

26 Use your place of birth as a password to protect the document. (AM3.3.4.1)

Task 2 Staff planner

In this task, you will cover the following skills:

- Create a form.
- Use form field options.
  - o Text form field.
  - o Drop-down menu.
- Protect a form.
- Edit a form.

- Merge cells in a table.
- Insert a field code.
- Delete a field code.
- Lock and unlock a field.
- Split cells in a table.

Scenario

While the Daniel Defoe document is with the Literary Group for checking, you have been tasked with drawing up the staff-evening rota for the next month. The rota is for part-time staff working on a very flexible basis. This means that the document is constantly being amended as staff change their working hours. To make the planning easier you can insert into a form all the names of the staff available at a particular time of day, and then re-select them as and when changes occur.

2.1 Create a form

Method

1 Open a New Blank Document by clicking on the icon.

2 To bring up the Forms toolbar, select **View** from the main menu bar, then select: **Toolbars**: **Forms**.

3 Run the pointer tool over the icons on the Forms Toolbar to see the options you have available.

Figure 2.1 Options on the Forms Toolbar

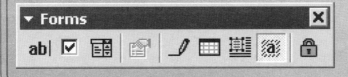

For this exercise, you will need to start with a table.

Method

1 From the Forms toolbar, select the **Insert Table** icon.

2 Select the maximum table size it will allow, i.e. a 4 x 5 table. Select by clicking in the bottom right-hand cell.

Handy Hint

If you know exactly the size of table you require, you can create a larger table, i.e. with more rows and columns, by holding down the left mouse button and dragging diagonally from the first cell until you have the size you want.

3 Key in the text for the table, as shown below. Use the tab key to move around the table.

	Week 1	Week 2	Week 3	Week 4
Monday	G Forrest	G Forrest	G Forrest	G Forrest
Tuesday	G Forrest	G Forrest	G Forrest	G Forrest
Wednesday	G Forrest	G Forrest	G Forrest	G Forrest
Thursday	G Forrest	G Forrest	G Forrest	G Forrest
Friday	G Forrest	G Forrest	G Forrest	G Forrest

To create an extra row, insert the cursor in the bottom right-hand cell and press the tab key.

2.2 Use form field options

Text form field and drop-down menu

The names of the members of staff that work evenings need entering into the form. These are:

- G Forrest
- R Solangi
- A Ahmed
- P Wong
- Y Brown
- H Johnson

Method

1 Click in the cell for Week 1, Monday.

2 On the **Forms** toolbar, click on: **Drop-Down Form Field**.

Figure 2.2 The Drop-Down Form Field on the Forms toolbar

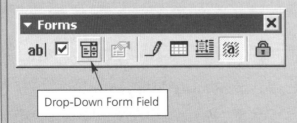

3 A shaded area will appear in the cell. Double-click in the shaded area and a **Drop-Down Form Field Options** dialogue box will appear (see Figure 2.3).

4 Key in the names of the staff in the **Drop-down item** box. After keying in each name, click on: **Add** (or press the **Enter** key) and the name will appear in the **Items in drop-down list** box.

Figure 2.3 Entering names in the Drop-down item box

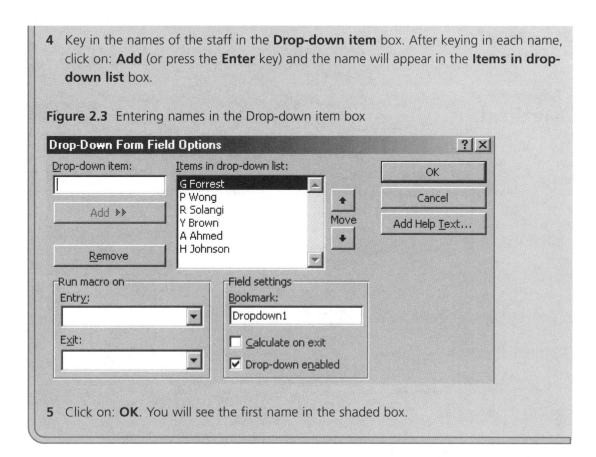

5 Click on: **OK**. You will see the first name in the shaded box.

Rather than spending time putting all the names into the other days and weeks, you can save time in the following way.

Method

1 Highlight the shaded cell by using the black pointer that appears at the left-hand side of the cell and clicking once.

2 Right-click once to access the pop-up menu, then select: **Copy**.

3 Highlight all the remaining cells up to Friday, Week 4.

4 Right-click once to access the pop-up menu, then select: **Paste**. Your table should look like the one below.

	Week 1	Week 2	Week 3	Week 4
Monday	G Forrest	G Forrest	G Forrest	G Forrest
Tuesday	G Forrest	G Forrest	G Forrest	G Forrest
Wednesday	G Forrest	G Forrest	G Forrest	G Forrest
Thursday	G Forrest	G Forrest	G Forrest	G Forrest
Friday	G Forrest	G Forrest	G Forrest	G Forrest

The table is still not working as a form with drop-down fields yet. You have to 'protect the form' to make the drop-down menus active.

Protect a form

1 If you have closed the Forms toolbar, access again by selecting **View**: **Toolbars**: **Forms**.

2 Click on the **Protect Form** icon (the icon that looks like a lock).

3 A drop-down arrow should appear. From this, you can select the staff names. Each of the cells in the table works independently, i.e. the arrow only appears in the cell when you click down into it.

Figure 2.4 Using the Protect Form icon to activate a drop-down menu

	Week 1	Week 2	Week 3	Week 4
Monday	G Forrest ±	G Forrest	G Forrest	G Forrest
Tuesday	G Forrest	G Forrest	G Forrest	G Forrest
Wednesday	P Wong	G Forrest	G Forrest	G Forrest
Thursday	R Solangi	G Forrest	G Forrest	G Forrest
	Y Brown			
Friday	A Ahmed	G Forrest	G Forrest	G Forrest
	H Johnson			

Edit a form

If you want to make changes to the drop-down menu, i.e. edit the form, you will have to unlock (unprotect) it by clicking once more on the Protect Form icon.

Merge cells in a table

The last row needs to be one column and the date and time fields need inserting.

1 Make sure that the document is unprotected by clicking on the **Protect Form** icon on the **Forms toolbar**.

2 Select the last row of the table by moving the mouse pointer to the left of the row, outside the table. When the cursor changes to a white arrow, click and the row should be selected.

3 Right-click to access the pop-up menu, then select: **Merge Cells**.

4 Click into the last row. It should now appear as one cell.

5 Key in the words 'Last updated by' followed by a colon.

6 Hold down the **Ctrl** key and press the **tab** key twice to insert two tabs.

7 Key in the word 'Date' followed by a colon.

8 Hold down the **Ctrl** key and press the **tab** key twice to insert two tabs.

9 Key in the word 'Time' followed by a colon.

You cannot insert tabs in tables unless you use both the Ctrl key and the tab key.

2.6 Insert a field code

Now that you have entered tab space between the texts on the last row, you can insert fields that automatically update whenever you open the document.

Method

To insert the date field:

1 Click in the table after the word 'Date:'.

2 Select: **Insert** from the main menu toolbar, then select: **Field** to access the **Field** dialogue box.

3 In **Categories**, select: **Date and Time**.

4 In **Field names**, select: **Date**.

5 Click on: **OK**. The date should now appear in the row.

Figure 2.5 Inserting the date field using the Field toolbar

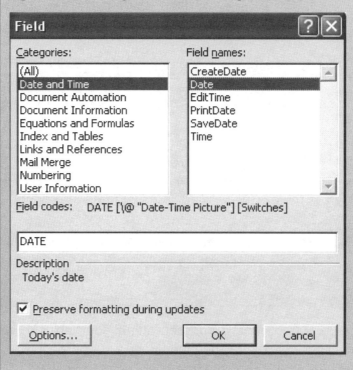

To insert the time field, repeat steps 1–3 above, then:

1 In **Field names**, select: **Time**.

2 Click on the **Options** button and in **Date-time formats** select: **h:mm:ss am/pm**.

Figure 2.6 Selecting the date-time formats

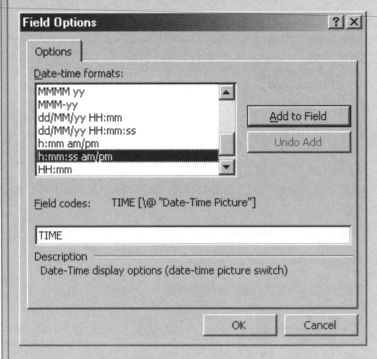

3 Click on: **Add to Field**.

4 Click on: **OK** to remove the Options dialogue box, then click on: **OK** to remove the Field dialogue box.

2.7 ## Delete a field code

Method

If you want to remove a field, for example if you inserted your field in the wrong position or selected the wrong field, you can delete it very easily. Double-click on the field to select it, then press the delete key on your keyboard.

You should now have the date and time showing in your table. You can see the fields if you click into either the date or the time – they are shaded.

2.8 ## Lock and unlock a field

To stop the fields automatically updating when the document is opened, i.e. so that you know when the table was last updated, you can lock the fields.

Method

Click in the 'Date:' field and press: **Ctrl + F11**. This action will lock the field.

If you right-click on the field now, you will see that Update Field is shaded out.

To unlock the field:

Check if you can update the field using right-click and selecting **Update Field**. Then re-lock the field.

2.9 Split cells in a table

It would also be useful to have an extra box in the table, for writing comments on the hard copy (the printout). To make the box, you can split the existing cells.

Method

1 Select all the cells that contain drop-down fields. Be careful not to select any other cells, e.g. the row and column headers.

2 Click on: **Table** on the main menu bar, then select: **Split Cells**. A Split Cells dialogue box should appear. In the **Number of columns** box, the number should be: 8. In the **Number of rows** box, the number should be: 5.

Figure 2.7 Splitting cells in the Split Cells dialogue box

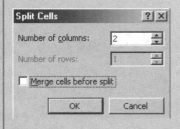

3 Deselect the **Merge cells before split** option by clicking to remove the tick. The **Number of Columns** changes to 2, the **Number of Rows** is shaded out.

4 Click on: **OK**.

You should now have an extra box next to each drop-down field.

There is always the possibility that someone else may update the document in your absence. You therefore need an area on the form where that person could insert his or her initials. The best way to do this is to insert a text field that the person updating can see.

1   Position the cursor to the right of the text 'Last updated by:'.

2   On the Forms toolbar, click on the **Text Form Field** icon.

Handy Hint

You should have a shaded area inserted after the colon. If you do not, click anywhere inside the table and then, on the **Forms** toolbar, click on the **Form Field Shading** icon.

If the **Last updated by** field has caused the time field to go to the next row, select the row and choose a smaller font size.

3   Save your document as **Staff rota**.

Practice Task   *Task 2*

These exercises are included to help the candidate in his or her training for the Advanced ECDL program. The exercises included in this material are not Advanced ECDL certification tests and should not be construed in any way as Advanced ECDL certification tests. For information about Authorised ECDL Test Centres in different National Territories, please refer to the ECDL Foundation website at **www.ecdl.com**.

You work in a restaurant and one of your responsibilities is to decide which set menu is to be offered. The set menus are already prepared, but the season, time of day and availability of fresh food will affect the choice of menu throughout the year. Ten set menus are rotated every 12 weeks.

1   Create a table that has 3 columns and 13 rows.

  ○ Label column 2, 'Lunchtime'. Label column 3, 'Evening'.
  ○ Label rows 2 to 13, 'Week 1', 'Week 2', etc.

2   Create a drop-down menu for Week 1, Lunchtime. The text for the list is: Menu 1, Menu 2, Menu 3, etc. up to Menu 10. (AM3.4.2.1) (AM3.4.2.2)

3   Duplicate (copy and paste) the list for the Evening of Week 1 and for Weeks 2 to 12, for both Lunchtime and Evening.

4   Save your work as: **Task 2 Answer**.

5   Insert a row at the top of the table.

Handy Hint

Table: Insert: Rows Above.

6   Merge the two adjacent cells at the top of column 1 and column 2, and insert a date field. (AM3.4.1.1) (AM3.3.2.1)

7   Insert one row at the bottom of the table. Merge the cells at the bottom of columns 2 and 3 and insert a field that shows the File Name.

8   Protect the form and check that your drop-down form fields are working. (AM3.4.2.4)

9 Using Pale Blue and Light Green colours, shade each Week row alternately.

Handy Hint

Format: Borders and Shading: Shading.

You need to unprotect the form first.

10 Apply the 'cake' (third selection) Art border to the page.

11 Insert a heading above the table, 'Set Menu Planner'.

Handy Hint

If you didn't leave room at the top of the page, move the table by dragging the square handle that appears in the top left-hand corner of the table when you run the cursor over the table.

For the heading:

o   choose Goudy Old Style, 24 pt
o   centre the heading
o   centre the text within the table.

Handy Hint

You can centre the heading text and the table text by holding down the Ctrl + A keys to select both, then clicking on the Center icon.

12 Change the height of the rows to 0.8 cm.

Handy Hint

Table Properties: Row, then specify the height (approximately 0.8 cm).

13 Insert a footer that will show the date the document was last saved.

Handy Hint

View: Header and Footer, then switch to Footer.

If you press the Enter key after you have inserted the field, the field will move up the page and out of the border area.

14 Save your work as: **Task 2 Answer**.

In this task, you will cover the following skills:

- Remove password protection.
- Modify footnotes and endnotes.
  - o Accessing footnote text.
  - o Amending footnote text.
  - o Accessing multiple footnote text.
- Change format and positioning of footnotes or endnotes.

- Create sections in a document.
  - o Break types.
  - o Section break types.
- Change column layouts.
- Insert a column break.
- Print more than one page per sheet.

Scenario

The document that you developed for the Literary Discussion Group in Task 1 has now been returned after checking, and there are amendments to be made.

3.1 | *Remove password protection*

The group thought that the password protection would cause problems if the people who had the password could not be contacted. To remove the password, you will need to open the document; you will be asked for the password.

Open your saved copy of Task 1. You will need the password to open the document.

If you have lost your work, or cannot remember the password to open your document, there is another copy on the CD in the 'Suggested Answers' folder. The file is named: Task 1 password protected. The password is 'password'.

Method

To resave the document without the password, i.e. to remove the password:

1 Click on: **File**, select **Save As**.

2 On the **Save As** menu bar, click on: **Tools**, then select **General Options**.

In the **Password to open** box, you will be able to see your password as asterisks, i.e. ******. **Delete** the asterisks.

3 Click on: **OK**.

4 Click on: **Save**.

The document should now be saved with the existing name but without the password protection. To check this, close the document and re-open it. If you were asked for the password, you need to repeat the above procedure.

Note: the method for modifying footnotes and endnotes is exactly the same.

The Literary group would like the footnotes amending.

Accessing footnote text

Method

As there are only two footnotes, you can use the following method. This method takes you directly to the footnote text:

1 Select: **View**: **Footnotes**, to access the View Footnotes dialogue box.

If you do not have any footnotes in your document, you will not be able to select this option.

Figure 3.1 The View Footnotes dialogue box

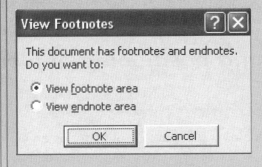

2 Select: **View footnote area**.

3 Click on: **OK**. The cursor will now move to the first footnote.

Amending footnote text

You can amend the text in the footnote just as you would in the main body of the document, i.e. you can select the text to change the font or font size. You can also add symbols and automatic numbering.

Method

1 Delete the word 'Roman' from the first footnote.

2 Click anywhere in the document, to exit the footnote area.

Accessing multiple footnote text

Method

If there had been more footnotes, it would have been easier to:

1 Click on: **Edit**.

2 Select: **Go To**.

3 From the **Go to what** box, select: **Footnote**.

Figure 3.2 Accessing footnotes from the Go to what box using Edit: Go To

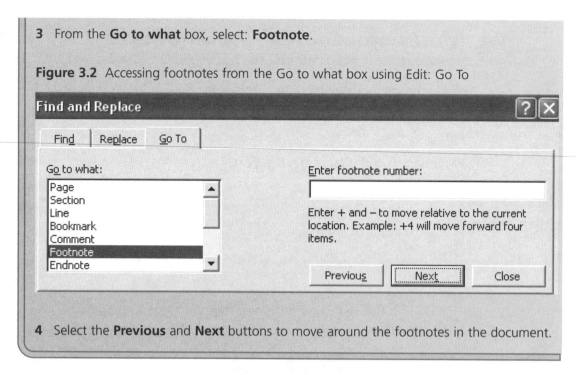

4 Select the **Previous** and **Next** buttons to move around the footnotes in the document.

Try this method now to see how it works.

Change format and positioning of footnotes or endnotes

On reflection, one of the footnotes would have been better as an endnote.

Method

1 Go to the second footnote, 'Mr Martin Creswell'. Right-click on the text.

Handy Hint

Take care that you don't click on a spelling error, underlined in red. Right-clicking on a spelling error brings up a different menu (see Figure 3.3). Word anticipates that you want to use Spellcheck and offers you this menu.

Figure 3.3 Be careful not to access the Spellcheck menu

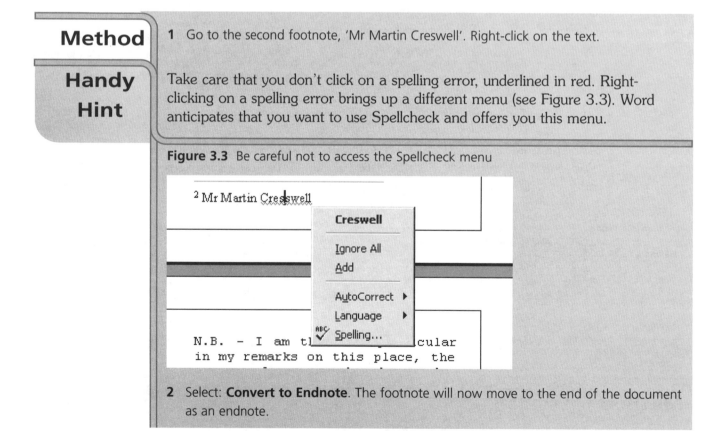

2 Select: **Convert to Endnote**. The footnote will now move to the end of the document as an endnote.

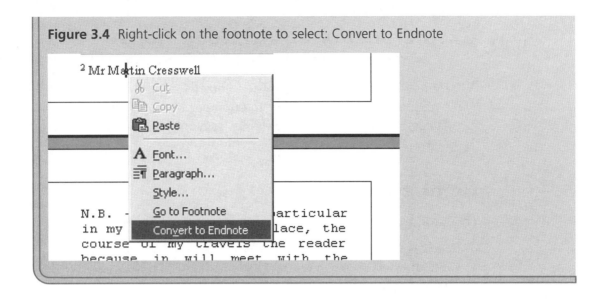

Figure 3.4 Right-click on the footnote to select: Convert to Endnote

Go to the end of the document to check that this has worked. You will see that the endnote marker in the main body of the text has automatically changed to: iii.

As illustrated below, you can also move the footnotes and endnotes around the document by highlighting the marker in the text, right-clicking and then dragging to the correct position.

Figure 3.5 Highlight the footnote or endnote marker, then right-click and drag to another position

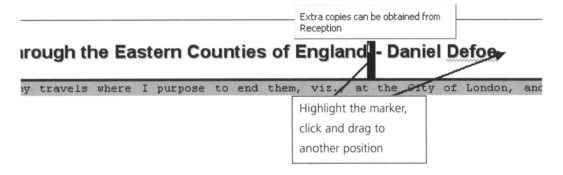

Method

1 Highlight the marker.

2 Click and drag the marker for the first Endnote, from its position after the word 'England' to the end of the heading, after the word 'Defoe'.

Handy Hint

If you find clicking and dragging a problem, don't forget that you can use Cut and Paste from the pop-up menu when you right-click, or from the icons on the standard toolbar.

Right-clicking on any of the listed endnotes at the end of the document gives you a pop-up menu. If you choose Go to Endnote, the cursor moves to the marker for that endnote. Try this on one of the endnotes.

A comment has come back from the Literary Group that the text looks too long. While nothing can be done about the number of words, the document can be formatted so that it appears in different sections and helps to break up the text for the reader.

Break types

There are three break types, i.e. what you want to break:

- Page break.
- Column break.
- Text wrapping break.

Section break types

In addition, there are four section break types, i.e. where you want the text to restart.

- Next page.
- Continuous (same page).
- (Next) even (numbered) page.
- (Next) odd (numbered) page.

Finding the point to insert the break

You are going to add a page break to force the text onto the next page. First, you need to find the point in the text where you want to insert the break.

Method

1 Select: **Edit**: **Find**, to access the Find and Replace dialogue box, then select the **Find tab**.

2 In the **Find what** box, key in: 'Several little'.

Figure 3.6 Using the Find what box in Edit: Find

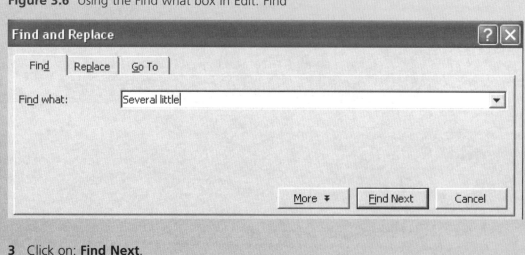

3 Click on: **Find Next**.

4 To close the **Find and Replace** dialogue box, click on: **Cancel**.

The cursor should now be at the start of the paragraph that begins 'Several little observations'. The words 'Several little' will be highlighted. Click down at the start of the paragraph before the word 'Several'.

Handy Hint

If you do not remove the highlighting before you put in the page break, you will lose the highlighted words.

Inserting the page break

Method

To insert the break you can either:

- Hold the **Ctrl** key and press the **Return** (**Enter**) key.

Or:

- Click on: **Insert**: **Break**, to access the Break dialogue box, select: **Page break**, then click on: **OK**.

The text should have moved to the top of the following page.

Adding column breaks

You are now going to convert a section of the text from 2 columns to a single column that spans the width of the page.

Method

1 Select the text from the top of this new page to the end of the paragraph numbered 3, i.e. to 'just above Gravesend'.

Handy Hint

The easiest way to do this is to hold down the shift key and use the arrow keys (down and right) to select the text. This gives you much more control.

2 You will now set the text into one column. This can be done in two ways:

- Select: **Format**: **Columns**, to access the Columns dialogue box. Select '1' in the Number of columns box, or click on the single column icon.
- Click on the **Column icon** on the standard toolbar and select: 1 column.

Figure 3.7 Using the Column icon to select 1 column

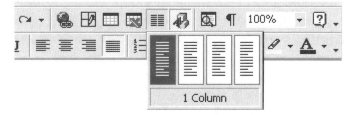

The text beginning 'Several little …' and the paragraphs numbered 1 to 3 should now run across the page.

If the last line that ends 'Gravesend' is force justified, i.e. if the words are spaced out across the page, press the Enter key (insert a return) after the word 'Gravesend' (see Figure 3.8).

If there is too much space between the paragraphs, click down in front of the word 'The' and press the backspace key. The text should move up the column (see Figure 3.8).

Figure 3.8 Move text up a column using the backspace key

> Press the Enter key here.

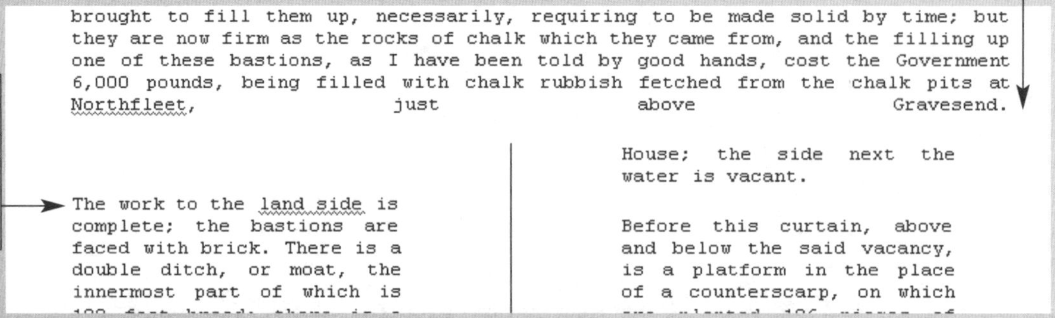

```
brought to fill them up, necessarily, requiring to be made solid by time; but
they are now firm as the rocks of chalk which they came from, and the filling up
one of these bastions, as I have been told by good hands, cost the Government
6,000 pounds, being filled with chalk rubbish fetched from the chalk pits at
Northfleet,            just            above            Gravesend.
```

> Press the Backspace key here to move the paragraph up the column.

```
The work to the land side is        House;  the  side  next  the
complete; the bastions are          water is vacant.
faced with brick. There is a
double ditch, or moat, the          Before this curtain, above
innermost part of which is          and below the said vacancy,
                                    is a platform in the place
                                    of a counterscarp, on which
```

Be careful not to press the backspace too many times – you will remove the section break instruction that you have just put in.

Repeat the above method with the text that starts 'From hence I went' (use Edit and Find to access this text). Start this on a new page (insert a page break) and apply one column format to the paragraph.

3.5 Change column layouts

Scroll through the document and format three more paragraphs. You can choose any three.

- Format the first paragraph to 1 column.
- Format the second paragraph to 2 columns.
- Format the third paragraph to 3 columns.

Triple-click on the text to select the whole paragraph.

Don't forget that you must highlight the section of text. If you do not, you will format the whole document. If you forget, the undo icon ↰ is the best option.

When you select the paragraph text, make sure that you highlight all the text in the paragraph, including the final full stop. If you do not, you will end up with one line of the paragraph detached from the rest of the text. Triple-clicking to select the paragraph will prevent this.

Insert a column break

One method of leaving space without starting a new page, for example for a picture, is to force the text to the top of the next column. To do this you can add column breaks.

Method

1 Insert the cursor on the first page at the front of the paragraph that starts, 'I set out the'.

2 Click on: **Insert**: **Break**, to access the Break dialogue box, then select: **Column break**. Do not select any Section break types – they are not appropriate. You want the text to start in the next column.

3 Click on: **OK**.

The text should move from column 1 to the top of column 2 on the first page. Column 1 should be blank after the word 'them' (see Figure 3.9).

Figure 3.9 Inserting a column break

```
I hope it will appear that I am        I set out the 3rd of April, 1722,
not  the  less,  but  the  more        going first eastward, and took
capable of giving a full account       what I think I may very honestly
of things, by how much the more        call a circuit in the very letter
deliberation I have taken in the       of it; for I went down by the
view of them, and by how much the      coast of the Thames through the
oftener I have had opportunity to      Marshes or Hundreds on the south
see them.                              side of the county of Essex, till
                                       I came to Malden, Colchester, and
                                       Harwich, thence continuing on the
                                       coast of Suffolk to Yarmouth;
                                       thence round by the edge of the
```

4 Save your work as: **Task 3**.

Print more than one page per sheet

Method

1 Select: **File**: **Print**, to access the Print dialogue box.

2 In **Page range**, click to select: **All**.

3 In the Zoom box, from the **Pages per sheet** drop-down menu, select: **4 pages**.

4 Click on: **OK**.

Figure 3.10 Printing 4 pages per sheet

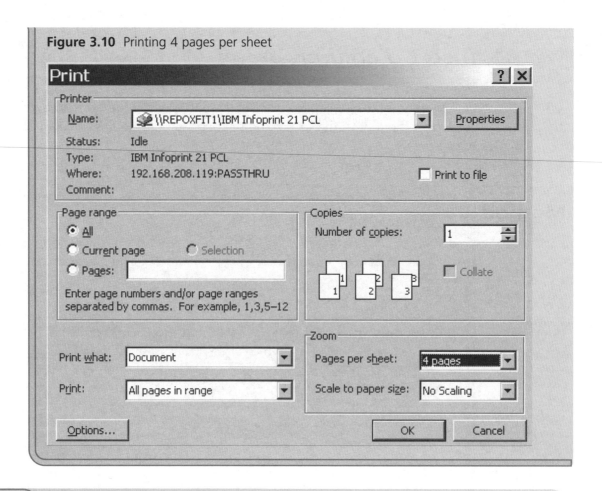

Practice Task   *Task 3*

These exercises are included to help the candidate in his or her training for the Advanced ECDL program. The exercises included in this material are not Advanced ECDL certification tests and should not be construed in any way as Advanced ECDL certification tests. For information about Authorised ECDL Test Centres in different National Territories, please refer to the ECDL Foundation website at **www.ecdl.com**.

Method

1   Remove the password from the document you saved as 'Task 1 Answer' at the end of Practice Task 1. (AM3.3.4.2)

2   Save your work as: **Task 3 Answer**.

3   Amend the footnote to read: See Leaflet 3. (AM3.3.3.2)

4   Convert the footnote to an endnote. (AM3.3.3.3)

5 Create a section break at the end of column 2 that forces columns 3 and 4 onto the next page. (AM3.2.3.1)

6 Change the Page Setup to Portrait. (AM3.1.1.7)

Handy Hint

Apply to 'Whole Document'.

7 Remove the column breaks. (AM3.2.4.5)

Handy Hint

There should be three column breaks to remove. Do not remove the page break.

8 Format the document to 2 columns. (AM3.2.4.2)

Handy Hint

Make sure that the position of the cursor on the page is away from the heading.

9 Increase the body text to 20 pt.

10 Reposition the sun image to the top of column 1, underneath the heading.

11 Increase the size of the image to fill the column width and to force the second subheading into column 2.

12 Reposition the watermark if it has moved off the page.

13 Add the following header: HOLIDAYS BY COACH. (Use: View: Header and Footer.)

- Use Arial Black font, 12 pt.
- Use a shadow effect on the font.
- Right align.

14 Print both pages onto one sheet of paper. (AM3.6.1.4)

15 Save your work as: **Task 3 Answer**.

Task 4 | *Advertisement flyer*

In this task, you will cover the following skills:

- Insert and delete text boxes.
  - Insert text boxes.
  - Delete text boxes.
  - Text wrapping.
  - Copy and position text boxes.
  - Inserting text.
- Link text boxes.
- Apply borders and shading to text boxes.
- Edit, move and re-size text boxes.
  - Move text boxes.
  - Change text box size.
  - Standardise text box size.
- Change text orientation.
  - Rotating text.

- Changing the shape of the rotated text box.
  - Formatting options.
- Apply animated text effects.
- Use text design gallery options.
  - The WordArt Toolbar.
- Use pre-defined shapes.
  - AutoShapes.
- Group and ungroup shapes.
  - Grouping.
  - Ungrouping.
  - Fix the position of grouped objects.
- Send shapes in front of or behind text; send shapes to back or to front.
- Change image borders.

Scenario

The next task is to produce an A4 flyer to advertise the next Literary Discussion Group meeting.

You will be using tools that are readily available through the Drawing Toolbar. Make sure that you have this toolbar showing at the bottom of your screen. If not:

- *Click on View: Toolbars: Drawing. The toolbar should appear at the bottom of the screen. The first item is Draw.*

Key in the following text on a new page. Leave the text at default. Leave one clear line space between each line of text.

> Literary Discussion Group
>
> Next Meeting 7.30pm
>
> (Put next Friday's date here)
>
> Tour Through the Eastern Counties of England
>
> Daniel Defoe
>
> Library Reading Room

4.1 | *Insert and delete text boxes*

Insert text boxes

After the line 'Tour Through the Eastern Counties of England', you are going to insert two text boxes.

1 Position the cursor on the blank line underneath the text.

2 Click on: **Insert**, then select: **Text Box**. The mouse cursor now changes to a black cross.

Another way of doing this is: on the **Drawing Toolbar**, click on the **Text Box** icon 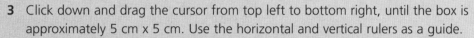.

3 Click down and drag the cursor from top left to bottom right, until the box is approximately 5 cm x 5 cm. Use the horizontal and vertical rulers as a guide.

Figure 4.1 Inserting a text box

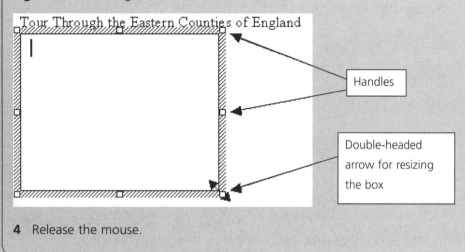

4 Release the mouse.

Delete text boxes

To delete the text box, right-click over one of the handles to select the box. From the pop-up menu, select: Cut.

The text box is selected when the border is shaded, as in Figure 4.1.

If you right-click anywhere else on the text box, other than over the handles, you will get different pop-up menus.

The I-beam cursor should be flashing in the text box. If the text box is sitting on top of the remaining text, you will need to wrap the text.

Text wrapping

To wrap the text:

1 Right-click on the shaded area around the text box to access the pop-up menu. (If you click inside the box, you will not get the Format Text Box option.)

Figure 4.2 Right-click to access the pop-up menu

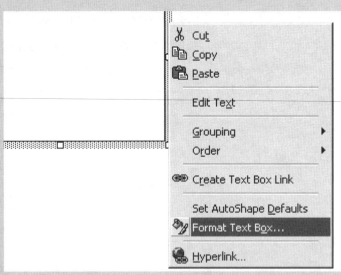

Another way of doing this is to select **Format** from the main menu toolbar, then select: **Text Box**.

2   Select: **Format Text Box**, to access the Format Text Box dialogue box.

3   Select the **Layout** tab.

4   Click on the **Advanced** button, to access the Advanced Layout dialogue box.

5   Select the **Text Wrapping** tab.

6   In Wrapping style, select **Top and bottom**. This option will force the text to flow to the top of the image and continue below it, i.e. the text will not flow over or under the image.

Figure 4.3 In Wrapping style, select Top and bottom in the Advanced Layout dialogue box

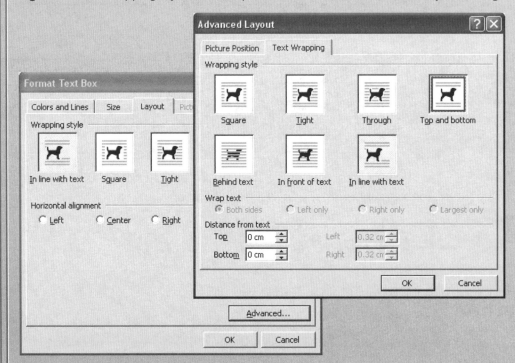

7   Click on: **OK** to close the **Advanced Layout** dialogue box, then click on: **OK** to close the **Format Text Box** dialogue box.

The text should now appear underneath the box.

Copy and position text boxes

Rather than repeat the above process to create a second identical box, you can make a copy of the original box.

1 Right-click on one of the text box handles, then select: **Copy**.

2 Click outside the box.

3 Right-click and select: **Paste**.

Note: if you do not click outside the box before selecting Paste, you will end up with the second text box inside the first.

Move the second text box somewhere to the right of the first one. It does not matter at this stage exactly where.

Click on the edge of the text box, avoiding the handles. Hold the left mouse button down and drag the box to the right.

Note: if you drag the handles, you will resize the box.

Figure 4.4 Click and drag to position the second text box

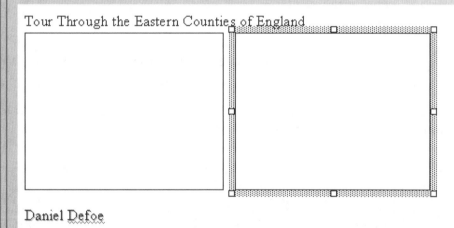

Inserting text

The first paragraph from the Daniel Defoe document is to be entered into the boxes.

1 From the folder: Task Files, open the file: **Text for Task 1**.

(This unformatted file is being used, rather than your saved Task 1 document, because the copy process will copy the formatting you have already applied.)

2 Triple-click on the first paragraph to select, then right-click to access the pop-up menu. Select: **Copy**.

3 Bring your A4 flyer back on screen. Unless you closed the file, you will be able to select the document from Window on the main toolbar.

4 Click in the first text box on the A4 flyer, then right-click and select **Paste**. The pasted text will be in one box, but you will not be able to see it all.

4.2 Link text boxes

To force the text into the next box, you need to create a link.

Method

1 Move the cursor over any of the square 'handles' on the first text box. A double-headed arrow should appear.

2 Right-click to access the pop-up menu, then select: **Create Text Box Link**. The cursor turns into a small jug.

3 Move the cursor over the second text box. As you do this, the jug tips and shows letters tumbling out (to indicate the remainder of the text).

4 Left-click in the second text box and the overflow text from the first text box should appear.

Don't worry at this stage that you cannot see all the text. The boxes are going to be resized and repositioned later.

4.3 Apply borders and shading to text boxes

To apply the same border and shading to both text boxes, you need to select them both before you apply the formatting.

Method

1 Click in the first text box. Hold down the **shift** key and click in the second text box. There should be shaded borders around both boxes. You can release the shift key.

2 Select: **Format**: **Borders and Shading**, to access the **Format Text Box** dialogue box.

3 Select the **Colors and Lines** tab.

Experiment with the options.

- Change the **Fill** colour – don't forget the **More Colors** option where you can choose a **Standard color** or create your own **Custom color**.
- Check the effect of selecting **Semitransparent** from the bottom of the Colors box, or to the right of Fill in the Format Text Box dialogue box.
- Change the colour, style and weight of the **Lines** – in this instance, the formatting is applied to the borders of the boxes.

Method

Figure 4.5 Experiment with the options using the Format Text Box dialogue box

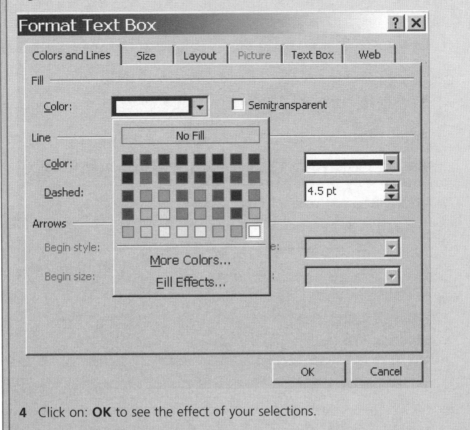

4 Click on: **OK** to see the effect of your selections.

5 Repeat the above method and make your final selections, as follows:

  o **Fill**: Light Turquoise.
  o **Line**: Light Green, Solid, 4.5 pt.

4.4 Edit, move and re-size text boxes

Move text boxes

Try moving the text boxes around the page – click and hold the mouse button down on the edge of the boxes and drag. You will see that no matter where the box is on the page, the text remains with the boxes, even if you put the second box in front of the first.

Change text box size

Now try changing the size of the text boxes. Make the first box bigger or smaller by clicking on any of the square 'handles' while holding down the left mouse button, and drag. The text will flow from one box to the other.

Standardise text box size

Now would be a good time to make both text boxes the same size.

Method

1 Select both the text boxes: click in the first box then hold down the Shift key and click in the second box.

2 Right-click to access the pop-up menu, then select: **Format Text Box**.

3 In the **Format Text Box** dialogue box, select the **Size** tab.

4 In **Height**, select: **6 cm**. In **Width**, select: **6 cm**.

Figure 4.6 Select text boxes size in the Format Text Box dialogue box

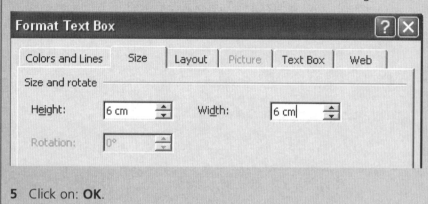

5 Click on: **OK**.

The boxes are now the same size. However, you can still change the size if you click and drag the handles.

The text should be Courier New, 10 pt. If the text is not this format, click in either box and select all the text by using Ctrl + A. Then format the text using the formatting toolbar.

4.5 Change text orientation

Rotating text

The Literary Group would like their name to run down the left-hand side of the flyer. This involves rotating the text. To be able to rotate or move text independently from the rest of the text on the page, you need to put the text to be rotated into a separate text box.

Method

1 Triple-click to select the text: **Literary Discussion Group**.

2 Click on **Insert** from the main menu bar, then select: **Text Box**.

Note: 'Literary Discussion Group' will appear in a text box but the box is too big and the wrong size. Do not make any changes to this text box yet.

3 Click on: **Format**, then select: **Text Direction**.

4 In the **Text Direction** dialogue box, select the first vertical option, i.e. the text reads from the bottom to the top (see Figure 4.7).

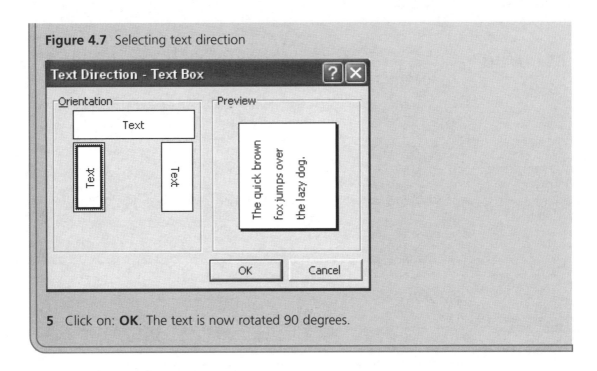

Figure 4.7 Selecting text direction

5 Click on: **OK**. The text is now rotated 90 degrees.

Changing the shape of the rotated text box

You are to change the shape of the box to 25 cm by 3 cm.

Method

1 Right-click over a box handle to access the pop-up menu. Select: **Format Text Box**. Click on the **Size** tab.

2 Set the box sizes: **Height**: **25 cm**; **Width**: **3 cm**.

3 Click on: **OK**.

Formatting options

The box is now the correct size but the text is too small, so you will now format the text.

Formatting text

Method

Select the text. You will notice when you click into the rotated box that the I-beam cursor is rotated 90 degrees. This means that you can format the text without changing the text direction back to horizontal. Make the following changes:

- Set the font to: **Arial, 48 pt, Bold**.
- Click on the **Center** icon on the **Formatting Toolbar** to centre the text within the box. The icons have been rotated, but they are still in the same position on the toolbar.

Formatting text box border

You will now change the colour and style of the line around the text box, and fill it with colour.

This is the same method that you used for the linked text boxes.

1 Select the text box by clicking inside.

2 Click on: **Format**: **Text Box**. In the Text Box dialogue box, in **Colors** and **Lines**, make the following selections:

   o **Fill**: Turquoise, semi-transparent.
   o **Line**: Blue, dash, 0.75 pt.

Hold the cursor still over the selections to access the pop-up text.

3 Click on: **OK**.

Formatting text colour

Make sure that the cursor is in the rotated text box area.

Change the colour of the text by first selecting the text (**Ctrl + A**) and then clicking on the **Font Color** icon **A** ▾ on the Formatting Toolbar. From the drop-down menu, select: **Indigo**.

4.6 Apply animated text effects

As the flyer is going to be emailed to existing members of the group, animated text effects can be applied. These will appear when the document is opened as an email attachment.

1 Select the title of the discussion, i.e. **Tour Through the Eastern Counties of England**.

2 On the main menu bar, click on: **Format**: **Font**, to access the Font dialogue box.

3 Select the **Text Effects** tab. Click on each of the animations in turn. You can view the effect in the **Preview** box at the bottom of the Font dialogue box.

4 Select: **Sparkle Text**.

Figure 4.8 Selecting animated text effects

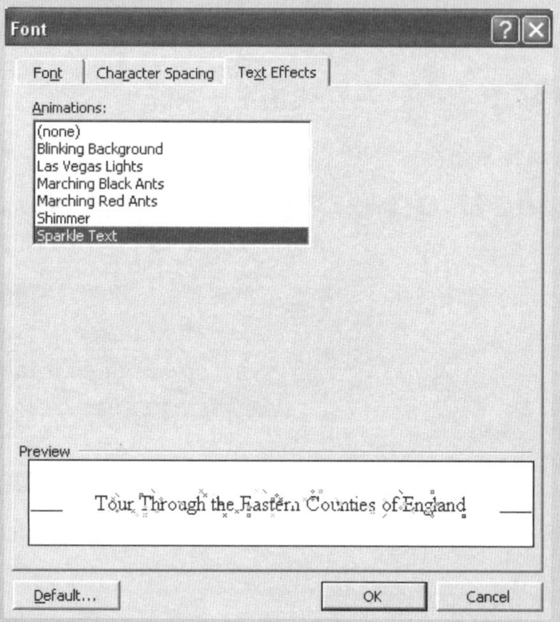

5 Click on: **OK**.

6 In the **Font** dialogue box, click on the **Font** tab. Now make the following changes:

- Font color: Red.
- Size: 36 pt.

Click on: **OK**.

7 Now change the case to upper case. Select: **Format**: **Change Case**, to access the Change Case dialogue box. Select: **UPPERCASE**.

Figure 4.9 Using the Change Case dialogue box

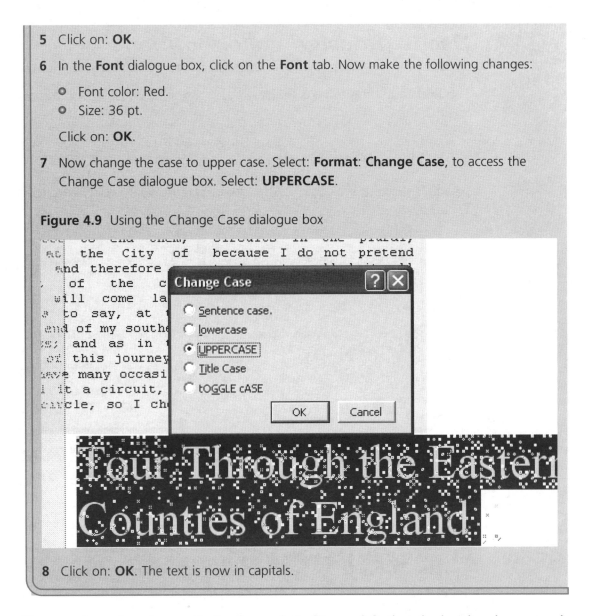

8 Click on: **OK**. The text is now in capitals.

You may have found, as with the example in Figure 4.9, that the heading has moved down the page and the text boxes have moved to accommodate the new text size. Don't panic! The easiest items to move on your document are the text boxes (because of the formatting applied earlier).

Method

1 Select both the linked boxes: click in one box then press Control and click in the second box.

2 Click on the edge of one of the boxes and drag them further down the page. The headline will now return to the top of the page.

A more fiddly method is to select the headline text and then left click and drag the text to the top of the page. You may find that, using this method, you still have to move the text boxes.

Use text design gallery options

The flyer is starting to take shape now, so we shall consider some more formatting options.

The WordArt Toolbar

To add 'Everyone Welcome' to the bottom of the flyer, we will use the WordArt Toolbar.

Method

1 Select: **View**: **Toolbars**: **WordArt**. The WordArt Toolbar will appear at the bottom of the screen.

2 Click on the first icon on the toolbar ◢.

3 Select the fifth option on the fourth row. Click on: **OK**. The **Edit WordArt Text** dialogue box will appear.

4 Key in the words: 'Everyone welcome'.

Figure 4.10 Keying in words in Edit WordArt Text

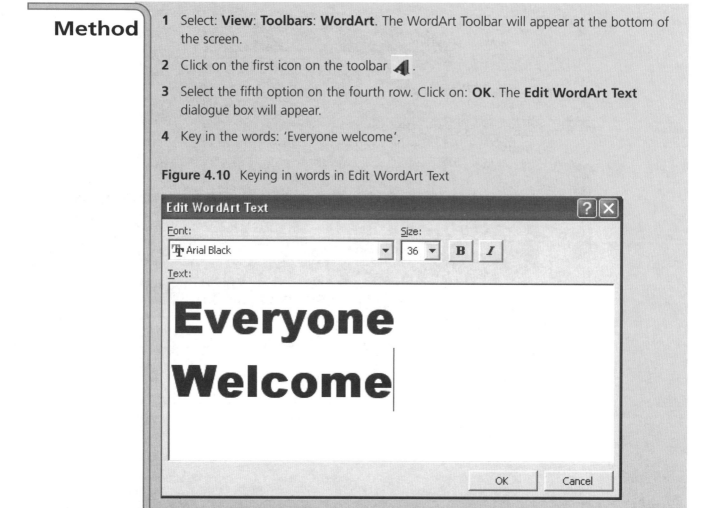

5 Click on: **OK** to return to the flyer. See what your selection looks like.

6 Click on the text and run the cursor over the WordArt toolbar.

Figure 4.11 The WordArt Toolbar

Experiment by selecting each of the icons in turn. Don't forget that you can click the 'undo' button on the main menu toolbar to return to your original selection.

The **Free Rotate** icon ⟲ works as follows: click on the icon, then click on the handles and drag round the centre axis.

Figure 4.12 Using the Free Rotate icon

Place the Free Rotate cursor over the round handles and drag

Click and drag the WordArt Toolbar to the bottom of the page to a position where it does not overlap the vertical text. To deselect the Free Rotate cursor, click on the Free Rotate icon on the toolbar.

4.8 Use pre-defined shapes

Included with Word are shapes that have been prepared for you to amend to your requirements. These options are called AutoShapes and are accessed through the Drawing Toolbar.

AutoShapes

Method

1 Select: **View**: **Toolbars**: **Drawing**.

2 Click on: **AutoShapes**.

3 Select **Block Arrows**, then click on: **Curved Left Arrow** (see Figure 4.13) and drag the cursor so that the curved arrow is in position on the right-hand side of the flyer, just above the WordArt text (see Figure 4.14).

Figure 4.13 Selecting arrow shapes in AutoShape

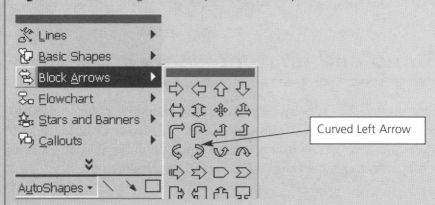

Curved Left Arrow

This takes practice. If you get it wrong, just delete the arrow with the delete key and start again.

4 Right-click on the arrow, then **Copy** and **Paste**, to create a second arrow. Position the arrows so that the lower arrow is in front of the higher arrow (see Figure 4.14).

5 On the **AutoShapes** drop-down menu, select: **Block Arrows**: **Left Arrow** (the second option on the first row). Click and drag to position this arrow to the left of the lower curved arrow (see Figure 4.14).

Figure 4.14 Click and drag on the arrows from the AutoShape drop-down menu to position in the document

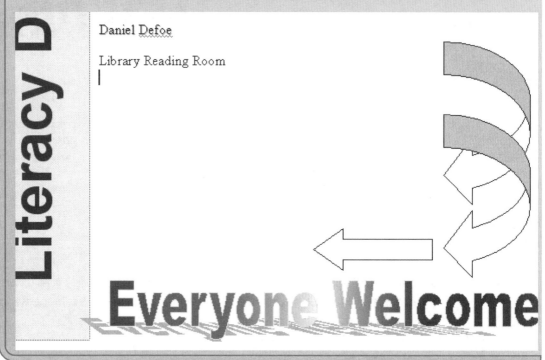

The block arrow pointing left needs to point to the words 'Library Reading Room'.

Method

1 Triple-click to select the text 'Library Reading Room' , then to place into a text box select: **Insert**: **Text box**.

2 Click on the text box and drag into position. You will need to modify the shape of the text box by dragging the handles.

3 Now remove the line border from around the text box: **Format**: **Text Box**, then click on the **Colors and Lines** tab. From the drop-down menu, select: **No Line**.

4.9 *Group and ungroup shapes*

You may find that your arrows have some element similar to the WordArt you chose for 'Everyone Welcome'. You can change this if you wish, but first it would be better to group the arrows so that you can format all three at once and stop the AutoShapes moving around the document independently.

Grouping

1 Hold down the **shift** key and select the two curved arrows and the left arrow by clicking on them in turn. (This is exactly the same method that you used to select the linked text boxes.)

2 Right-click: this should be a quick click to get the correct pop-up menu. Select: **Grouping**, then select: **Group**.

Figure 4.15 Fixing the position of AutoShapes using Grouping: Group

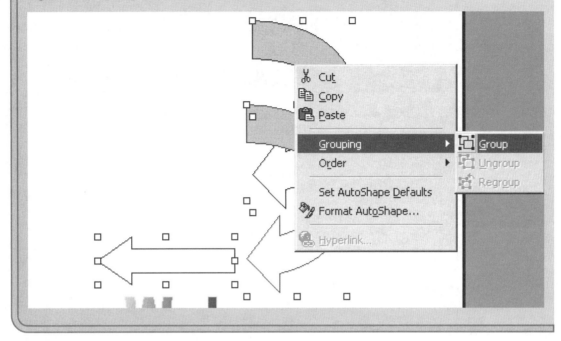

Ungrouping

If you later wanted to Ungroup the AutoShapes, you follow the same method, selecting **Grouping**, then select: **Ungroup**.

If you find right-clicking particularly difficult when handling AutoShapes, left-click in the AutoShape and make the selections from the Drawing toolbar. Click on the Draw drop-down menu to access the Group and Ungroup options.

You should have one set of handles around the outside of all three AutoShapes. These Grouped AutoShapes now work just as any other image or picture until they are Ungrouped.

Fix the position of grouped objects

The AutoShapes will still move around the document as you make amendments to, for example, the text or the text boxes. The way to stop this happening is to format the AutoShapes (objects) so that they do not move with the text.

Method

1 Click on the arrows, hold down the Shift key and click on the 'Everyone Welcome' text.

2 Move the cursor over a handle and right-click, select: **Format Object** to access the Format Object dialogue box. Another way to access the Format Object dialogue box is to left-click and select: **Format**: **Object** on the main menu bar.

3 Select the **Layout** tab, then click on the **Advanced** button. The **Advanced Layout** dialogue box appears.

4 Click on: **Picture Position** tab.

5 Under **Options**, deselect the **Move object with text** box.

Figure 4.16 Fixing the position of grouped objects using the Advanced Layout dialogue box

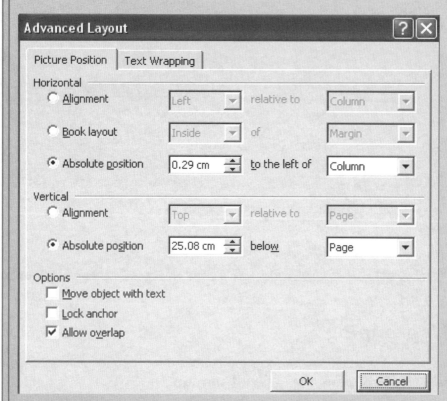

6 Click on: **OK** twice to remove the dialogue boxes. You may need to re-position the AutoShapes after clicking on the second OK.

You won't see any obvious changes but if you insert any line spaces now, or re-size the text boxes, the 'Everyone Welcome' text and the arrows will not move.

You will now make some changes to the font and add a second shape – the Cloud Callout – to the flyer.

Method

1 Change the 'Library Reading Room' and 'Daniel Defoe' text to Times New Roman, 18 point.

2 Click and drag the text box and/or the WordArt/AutoShape into position.

3 You will add the Cloud Callout to the end of the extract text in the boxes. Click on the **AutoShapes** drop-down menu from the Drawing toolbar, then select: **Callouts**: **Cloud Callout**.

Group and ungroup shapes

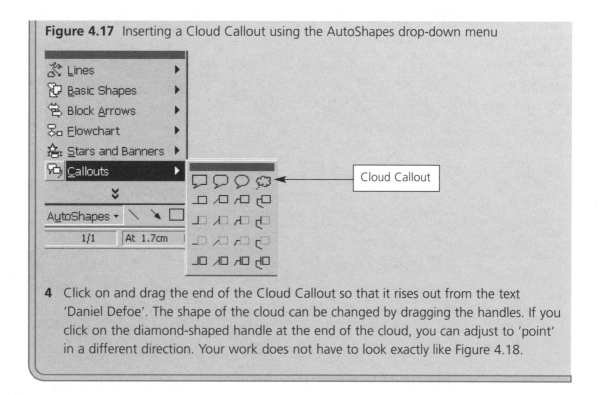

Figure 4.17 Inserting a Cloud Callout using the AutoShapes drop-down menu

4   Click on and drag the end of the Cloud Callout so that it rises out from the text 'Daniel Defoe'. The shape of the cloud can be changed by dragging the handles. If you click on the diamond-shaped handle at the end of the cloud, you can adjust to 'point' in a different direction. Your work does not have to look exactly like Figure 4.18.

4.10   *Send shapes in front of or behind text; send shapes to back or to front*

To ensure that the cloud is on top of the text boxes, i.e. that it is in front of the text, you can apply ordering options to pre-defined shapes.

Method

1   Click on the Cloud Callout.

2   Click on: **Draw**.

3   Select: **Order**.

You will see a range of options. What you have on screen will determine which of the options will have an effect. If your cloud is behind the text, you need to select **Bring in Front of Text**.

Figure 4.18 Setting an AutoShape in front of text using Draw: Order

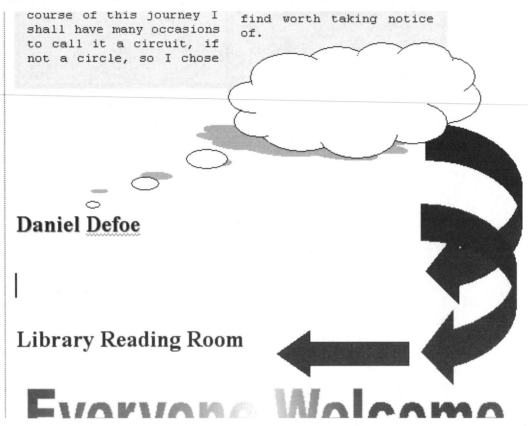

Try the options out on the Cloud Callout:

- Bring to Front.
- Send to Back.
- Bring Forward.
- Send Backward.
- Bring in Front of Text.
- Send Behind Text.

4.11 *Change image borders*

The Cloud Callout may have picked up some formatting, for example, the same formatting as the other AutoShapes. You need to change the format of the cloud to a white fill with black lines.

Method

1 Right-click over one of the handles, then select: **Format AutoShape: Colors and Lines**.

2 Select the following options:

- **Fill**: White.
- **Line**: Black, solid, 1 pt.

3 Format the 'Next Meeting' and 'Date' text to 26 pt and centred.

4 Check that the different elements are still in place. If not, select them and drag into position.

5 Save the document as: **Flyer**.

You may have noticed that the 'formatting' dialogue boxes, e.g. Format Object, Format Picture, Format Text Box and Format AutoShape, are all fairly similar in that they contain the same tab headings. The content of these headings are explored as you work on different tasks throughout the book.

You are not restricted to formatting and making modifications using the above dialogue boxes: you can also add and modify borders to pictures using Borders and Shading, for example.

Method

1   Open a new blank document and insert an image from ClipArt, i.e. **Insert**: **Picture**: **ClipArt**.

2   Make a selection from the **Photographs** category. If you do not have this category, make a selection from any of the other categories.

   You should have an image on-screen with black square handles.

3   Right-click on the image and select: **Borders and Shading**. The Borders dialogue box appears.

4   Make the following selections:

   o   **Setting**: Box
   o   **Style**: see Figure 4.19
   o   **Color**: Violet
   o   **Width**: 6pt

   (Note: Not all the Style options have the choice of 6 pt; if this is not available, choose the widest width available.)

5   Make sure that the **Apply to**: box has **Picture** selected.

Figure 4.19 Adding a border to a picture using the Borders dialogue box

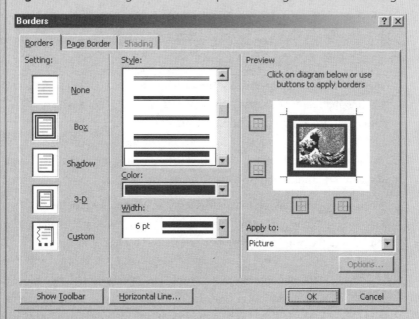

6   Click on: **OK**. Your picture should now have a border around it.

7   Amend the border by right-clicking on the picture, then select: **Borders and Shading**. Change the **Setting** to **Shadow**. Click on: **OK**.

You can also apply formatting options to the picture using the Picture toolbar that appears when you insert the picture. Click on the picture and check out the effects that using Image Control, Contrast, Brightness, etc. has on the picture.

When using the cropping tool, don't forget to position the cursor over the handles on the picture. To reset the picture to the original form, click on the final icon on the toolbar: Reset Picture.

Practice Task | *Task 4*

These exercises are included to help the candidate in his or her training for the Advanced ECDL program. The exercises included in this material are not Advanced ECDL certification tests and should not be construed in any way as Advanced ECDL certification tests. For information about Authorised ECDL Test Centres in different National Territories, please refer to the ECDL Foundation website at **www.ecdl.com**.

You are going to create an A4 handout on the *Phantom of the Opera* by Gaston Leroux.

The flyer is going to be portrait, with one image and a border. To give you a starting point, look at the suggested Task 4 Answer on page 152. Your completed document may look quite different from the one in the book: this is not important, provided that you have used all the Word functions that the Task requires.

WordArt and Drawing Tools will be used for the subheading and the text border:

○ Subheading: 'Prologue'
○ Text border: 'In which the author of this singular work informs the reader how he acquired the certainty that the opera ghost really existed'

Below is the main body of text, which will be inserted in to linked text boxes. The file is stored in your Task Files folder as: Opera Text.

The Opera ghost really existed. He was not, as was long believed, a creature of the imagination of the artists, the superstition of the managers, or a product of the absurd and impressionable brains of the young ladies of the ballet, their mothers, the box-keepers, the cloak-room attendants or the concierge. Yes, he existed in flesh and blood, although he assumed the complete appearance of a real phantom; that is to say, of a spectral shade.

When I began to ransack the archives of the National Academy of Music I was at once struck by the surprising coincidences between the phenomena ascribed to the 'ghost' and the most extraordinary and fantastic tragedy that ever excited the Paris upper classes; and I soon conceived the idea that this tragedy might reasonably be explained by the phenomena in question. The events do not date more than thirty years back; and it would not be difficult to find at the present day, in the foyer of the ballet, old men of the highest respectability, men upon whose word one could absolutely rely, who would remember as though they happened yesterday the mysterious and dramatic conditions that attended the kidnapping of Christine Daae, the disappearance of the Vicomte de Chagny and the death of his elder brother, Count Philippe, whose body was found on the bank of the lake that exists in the lower cellars of the Opera on the Rue-Scribe side. But none of those witnesses had until that day thought that there was any reason for connecting the more or less legendary figure of the Opera ghost with that terrible story.

GASTON LEROUX

1   Open a new document and create three text boxes, size 9 cm x 7 cm. (AM3.4.3.1)

Handy Hint

Create box 1, copy and paste to produce box 2 and 3. Arrange the boxes as in the suggested answer on page 152.

Set Zoom to: Whole Page.

2   Insert the file: Opera Text into the first text box.

3   Link the text boxes and drop the text into the remaining 2 text boxes. (AM3.4.3.4)

4   Apply Lavender shading to the boxes. (AM3.4.3.3)

5   Apply a Dash Dot border, Plum colour, 1.5 pt weight.

6   At the top of the page as the heading, key in: Phantom of the Opera. Use sentence case. Format as follows:

   o   Font: GiGi
   o   Style: Bold
   o   Size: 48 pt
   o   Colour: Red
   o   Effect: Emboss
   o   Underline: Dotted
   o   Align: Centre

7   Using WordArt (select the last option on the third row), insert in uppercase the word: PROLOGUE. Format to: Showcard Gothic font, 40 pt. Position the WordArt centrally below the heading. (AM3.1.1.8)

The remainder of the text you are going to run around the outside of the page to form the border.

8   Using a text box, insert in uppercase the words: IN WHICH THE AUTHOR OF THIS SINGULAR WORK INFORMS.

Handy Hint

From the Zoom drop-down menu, select: Whole Page.

9   Apply the following formatting:

   o   Chiller font, 36 pt, bold.
   o   Choose a deep red colour from More Colors: Standard.
   o   Order the text box to: Send Behind Text.
   o   Remove the border (if you have one).
   o   Rotate the text so that the base of the letters is to the right. (AM3.1.1.7). Resize the box to accommodate the text.
   o   Place this text box down the left-hand side of the page.

10 Using a text box, insert the words: THE READER HOW HE ACQUIRED. Place this text box at the top of the page.

Select the previous text box, copy and paste, change the wording, rotate, resize and reposition. This will save you the work of formatting the font again. (AM3.4.3.2)

11 Using a text box, insert the words: THE CERTAINTY THAT THE OPERA GHOST REALLY EXISTED. Rotate the text so that the base of the letters is to the left. Place this text box down the right-hand side of the page.

12 In the top corners of the page, to indicate the direction of the border text, insert: AutoShapes: Bent Arrow. (AM3.4.5.3). Fill each of the corner arrows with the same colour as the border text. (AM3.4.5.1)

Copy and rotate the first arrow to produce the second arrow. To do this, click on the first arrow, then select: Draw: Rotate or Flip: Rotate Right.

13 Search for Eiffel Tower images in ClipArt. Select the first image with the lilac background.

  - Format the picture to: Square layout.
  - Position in the bottom right-hand corner of the page.
  - Remove the sky and the pale yellow base colour. (AM3.4.5.6)

Ungroup the image, click anywhere on the page away from the image, click on the portion you want to delete. This is much easier to do if you Zoom the page to 200%.

14 Reformat the image as a group.

Use the white pointer tool from the Drawing toolbar and draw a box (a marquee) around the separate parts to select them all.

15 Change the font in the body text boxes to: Arial, 12 pt.

Select the text in all three boxes by clicking in the first box and using Ctrl + A keys.

16 Re-position the text boxes so that they form a square with the image. (See suggested answer.) (AM3.4.3.2)

17 Apply to the heading the text effect: Blinking Background. (AM3.1.1.2)

18 Save your work as: **Task 4 Answer**.

The Narrowboat Company

In this task, you will cover the following skills:

- Convert text into a table.
- Sort data in a table.
  - o Alphabetic or numeric.
  - o Ascending or descending order.
- Perform addition calculations on numeric data in a table.
- Create a chart
  - o Create a chart from a table.
  - o Create a chart from pasted spreadsheet data.
- Modify an embedded worksheet.

- Change the formatting of a chart.
  - o Modify a chart created from a table.
  - o Modify a chart created from pasted worksheet data.
- Change the position of a chart in a document.
- Add and update an image, table or worksheet caption.
- Add a numbered caption to an image, figure, table or worksheet.
  - o Update existing captions.

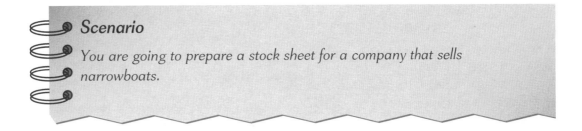

Scenario

You are going to prepare a stock sheet for a company that sells narrowboats.

5.1 Convert text into a table

From your Task Files folder, open the file: **Task 5**. Click on the Show/Hide icon ¶. You will see that the page contains a block of tabbed text that could be displayed as a table.

Method

1 Select the text from 'LOCATION' to '54,750'.

2 Click on: **Table** on the main menu toolbar, then select: **Convert**: **Text to Table**. The Convert Text to Table dialogue box will appear.

Figure 5.1 The Convert Text to Table dialogue box

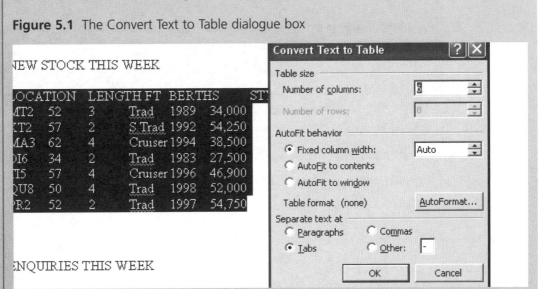

If you have selected the text correctly, Word should have recognised the Table size as 6 columns and 8 rows. If not, you need to amend the number of columns box.

3 Click to select: **Fixed column width**. This option displays the table across the full width of the page.

4 Click on: **OK**.

5 Repeat the above procedure on the smaller section of text below the heading 'ENQUIRIES THIS WEEK'. This time, in the Convert Text to Table dialogue box, select: **AutoFit to contents**. This option displays the table to fit the longest length of text in the column.

The figures have been entered incorrectly. Click in the table and amend the figures as below.

Figure 5.2 Amend the figures in the table as shown

ENQUIRIES THIS WEEK

Traditional	12
Semi Traditional	21
Cruiser	18

5.2 Sort data in a table

One of the most important questions customers ask when buying a narrowboat is what is the size. To make answering enquiries more efficient, the table needs to be sorted into order of length.

Method

1 Click anywhere in the table.

2 Click on: **Table** on the main menu toolbar, then select: **Sort**. The Sort dialogue box will appear (see Figure 5.3).

3 From the **Sort by** drop-down menu, select: **column 2** and the **Descending** radio button.

4 There is a header row on the table, i.e. LOCATION, LENGTH FT, etc. To prevent Word trying to sort the top (header) row of text with the rest of the table, click on the radio button **Header row**. You will see that in the Sort by drop-down menu, you now have the heading of the row you are sorting, i.e. LENGTH FT.

The price can be sorted at the same time.

1 From the **Then by** drop-down menu, select: **PRICE £**. You will notice that Word automatically recognises whether you have text or numbers in the column when the radio button Header row is selected.

2 Select: **Ascending**.

3 Click on: **OK**.

Figure 5.3 Using the Sort dialogue box to sort data in a table

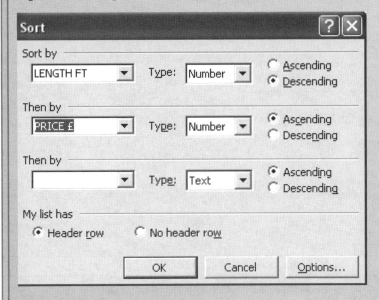

The two 57 ft boat prices should now be listed in ascending price order.

Perform addition calculations on numeric data in a table

5.3

The Narrowboat Company has bought more boats than usual this week. As all the stock is bought using a bank overdraft, a check needs to be made to ensure that the budget of £300,000 is kept to.

Large amounts of calculation data should be made using a spreadsheet, but you can perform a quick calculation using Word. The calculation must be done inside the table, so you need to create another row to accommodate this.

1 Click in the cell at the end of the last row, i.e. the bottom right-hand corner.

2 Press the **Tab key**, or click on: **Table**: **Insert**: **Rows Below**.

You should now have a new row.

In the first column, key in the text: 'VALUE OF NEW STOCK'.

Figure 5.4 Key in the text: VALUE OF NEW STOCK

LOCATION	LENGTH FT
MA3	62
TI5	57
KT2	57
MT2	52
PR2	52
QU8	50
DI6	34
VALUE OF NEW STOCK	

The text 'VALUE OF NEW STOCK' is squashed into one column. To spread the text along the row you can merge the cells in the adjacent columns.

Method

1   Highlight the text in column 1 and the two blank cells to the right.

Figure 5.5 Highlight columns 1 to 3

DI6	34	2	Trad	1983
VALUE OF NEW STOCK				

2   Click on: **Table: Merge Cells**.

The text 'VALUE OF NEW STOCK' should now appear in one row.

Handy Hint

Always sort your table before you perform any merge operations.

Note: you cannot sort merged cells. It is important to remember that if you want to sort a table after you have merged cells, you must select only the unmerged rows that you want to sort, not the whole table. This will mean that you have to perform several sort operations to sort the table. If you try to sort the whole table, Word will move the merged cells to the bottom of the table.

To insert the calculation:

Method

1   Click in the last cell in the PRICE £ column, on the VALUE OF NEW STOCK row.

2   Click on: **Table: Formula**. The Formula dialogue box appears.

Perform addition calculations on numeric data in a table

The default **Formula** is: =SUM(ABOVE). You can make further selections using the **Paste function** drop-down menu but not all the selections are appropriate (see Figure 5.6). If you make an obviously wrong selection, you will get the message: **!Syntax Error** in the selected cell of the table.

Figure 5.6 The Formula dialogue box

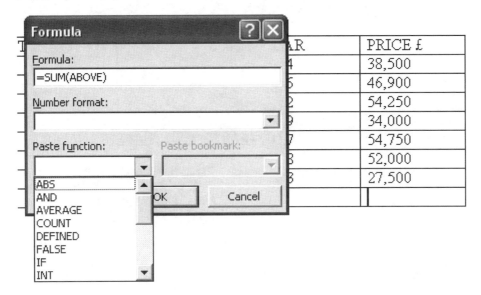

You can also change the number format: have a look at the options in the **Number format** drop-down menu. The default is appropriate for this document, but you do have other choices.

Leave the dialogue box at default and click on: **OK** to total the column. The total is greater than the overdraft limit! Fortunately, the company has received an unusual amount of enquiries for boats this week. This good news would look even better if presented as a graph.

5.4 Create a chart from a table or pasted spreadsheet data

Create a chart from a table

The graph can be created from the ENQUIRIES THIS WEEK table.

Method

1 Select the data in the table by either of the following methods:

- highlight using the mouse
- click in the table, then select: **Table**: **Select**: **Table**.

2 Click on: **Insert** from the main menu bar, then select: **Picture**: **Chart**.

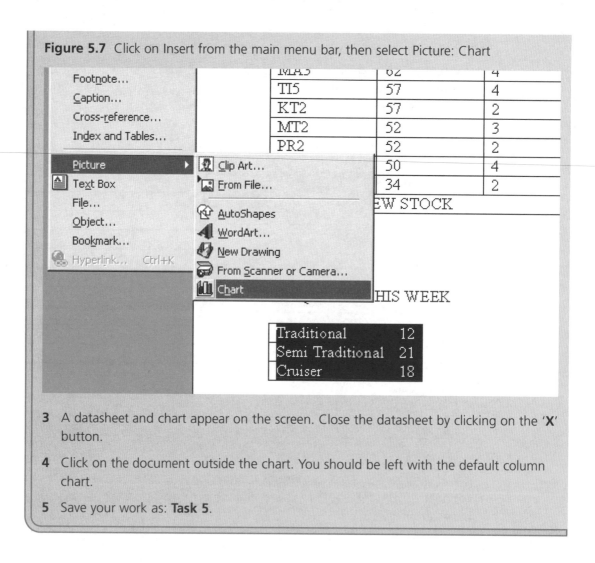

Figure 5.7 Click on Insert from the main menu bar, then select Picture: Chart

3 A datasheet and chart appear on the screen. Close the datasheet by clicking on the 'X' button.

4 Click on the document outside the chart. You should be left with the default column chart.

5 Save your work as: **Task 5**.

Create a chart from pasted spreadsheet data

The above chart has been created in Word. You can also create charts from Excel. This involves putting the data into an Excel spreadsheet and then copying the data into Word.

Copying data from Excel into Word

Method

1 Open: **Excel**.

2 Key in the following data as illustrated in Figure 5.8:

Traditional 18
Semi Traditional 24
Cruiser 52

3 Highlight to select the cells from A1 diagonally to B3.

4 Right-click and select: **Copy**.

Figure 5.8 Key in the data in Excel, then right-click and select: Copy

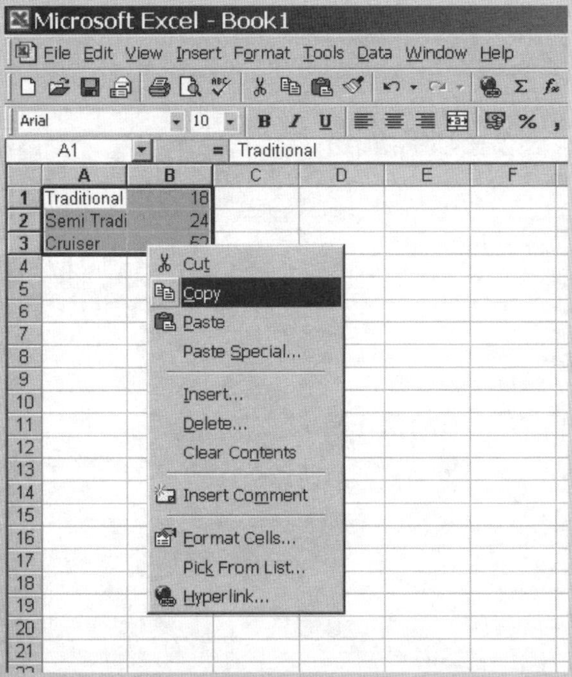

5 Open a new Word document.

6 Select: **Edit**: **Paste Special**. A Paste Special dialogue box appears.

7 In the **As**: box, select: **Microsoft Excel Worksheet Object**.

8 Click on: **OK**.

Note: it is important that you select Paste Special and not simply Paste. Paste Special pastes (embeds) the spreadsheet into the document, not just the data. If you double-click on the embedded spreadsheet, you will see that the row and column headings are visible.

Also, if you click to select the **Paste link** radio button, when you double-click on the embedded worksheet this will link you back to the original Excel Worksheet. While this is a useful tool, it is not always appropriate and can prove very frustrating as you jump unnecessarily from Word to Excel.

Creating a chart from pasted Excel data

To create a chart from this data:

Method

1 Double-click on the embedded worksheet.

2 Select: **Insert**: **Chart**.

3 Select: **Column**: **Next**: **Next**: **Next**: **Finish** (see Figure 5.9 and 5.10).

Figure 5.9 Select the chart type

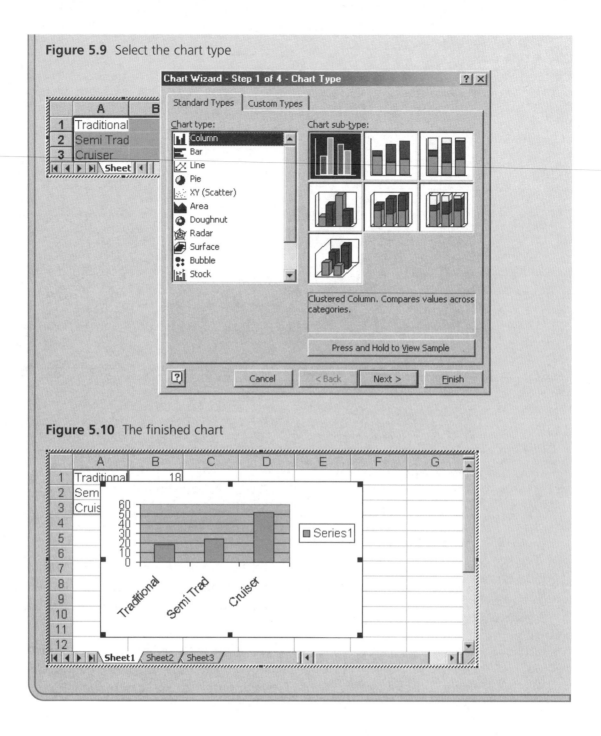

Figure 5.10 The finished chart

You should be able to see the chart in the embedded worksheet. To see the entire chart, you can drag out the bottom right-hand handle of the worksheet.

Click down outside the worksheet to deselect it.

Create a chart from a table or pasted spreadsheet data

5.5 Modify an embedded worksheet

If you use the above method to create a table from data pasted in Word from an Excel worksheet, and then need to change the data, double-click on the data. Excel formatting icons appear at the top of the screen and the embedded worksheet is made available for editing.

If the chart is covering the numbers, you will need to move it to one side by clicking on the chart (make sure that you have the 4-headed arrow) and dragging to a new position.

Method

1 Make the following changes. You will see the chart update as you are inputting the new data:

- Traditional: 12
- Semi Traditional: 21
- Cruiser: 18

2 Save your work as: **Task 5a**.

5.6 Change the formatting of a chart created from a table or pasted spreadsheet data

Open: **Task 5** again and double-click on the chart. The main menu toolbar will show tools for formatting the chart.

The various elements of the chart can be selected from the drop-down menu (see Figure 5.11). These can then be formatted by clicking on the icons. If you click on the drop-down menu at the end of the toolbar, you will see more icons, for example, Fill and Gridlines.

Figure 5.11 Using the Chart Toolbar to format a chart

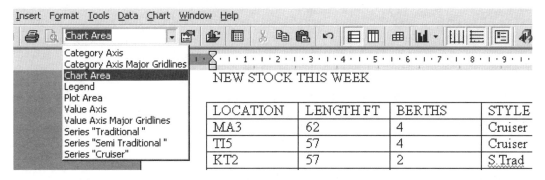

Try some of the options to see the effects.

If you make several changes that you don't like, and the Undo button won't undo any more, you can close without saving and reopen the file.

The Narrowboat Company always use pie charts, so the column chart needs to be changed accordingly.

Modifying chart type

Method

1 To select the chart, double-click on the chart. You should have a shaded box around the chart and a toolbar at the top of the screen with chart formatting icons.

2 Click on the **Chart Type** icon ![icon], then from the drop-down menu select: **Pie Chart**. (You may have to click on the drop-down menu at the end of the toolbar to see the Chart Type icon.)

Note: make sure that you have not selected any of the individual elements of the table, e.g. a single column, because you will end up with just that column shown as a pie chart.

You should get a chart that looks like this:

Figure 5.12 Changing the table to a pie chart

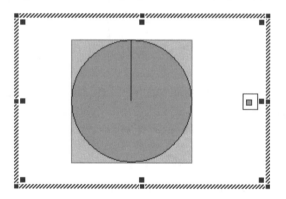

The reason the table looks wrong as a pie chart is because the software reads the data from left to right for the table, i.e. in rows. You need the software to read the data in columns to present it correctly in a pie chart.

Method

On the Chart Toolbar, click on the **By Column** icon ![icon].

Change the position of a chart in a document and add figures

5.7

Now delete the 'ENQUIRIES THIS WEEK' table from the page by clicking in the table, then selecting: **Table: Delete: Table**.

Deleting the table will not affect your graph as the data required to produce the graph is now stored in the datasheet table. To see the datasheet, double-click on the chart then click on: **View: Datasheet**.

Changing the chart position
Now the table has been deleted, the graph can be moved into position underneath the heading 'ENQUIRIES THIS WEEK'.

Method

1 Click once in the graph – you should get a box with square handles.

2 Click on the **Align Left** icon on the formatting toolbar.

Handy Hint

If you double-click to select the chart (i.e. so that the chart has a shaded border), you will not have access to the formatting toolbar.

Adding figures to the pie chart
The pie chart does not make any sense without figures. To add figures to the chart:

Method

1 Double-click on the pie chart to select it.

2 Double-click on the pie chart area. You should get the **Format Data Series** dialogue box.

3 Select the **Data Labels** tab.

4 Click on the radio button **Show value**. This will pick up the data from the datasheet.

Figure 5.13 Adding data to a pie chart using the Format Data Series dialogue box

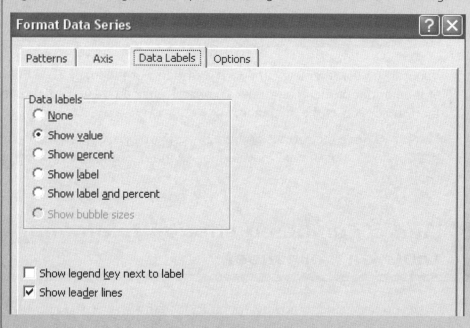

5 Click on: **OK**. The number of enquiries should appear next to the appropriate pie segment.

5.8 Add and update an image, table or worksheet caption

At the top of the document is an image that the Narrowboat Company uses as a logo. The caption underneath the image needs to be updated.

Method

1 Right-click on the image, then from the pop-up menu select: **Caption**. A Caption dialogue box appears.

2 Click on: **New Label**. A New Label dialogue box appears.

3 In the **caption** box, key in: **The Narrowboat Company**.

4 Click on: **OK**.

Figure 5.14 Changing a picture caption using the Caption dialogue box

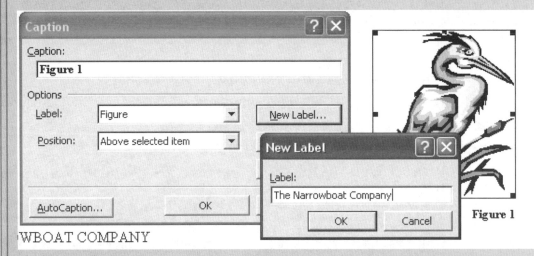

5 From the **Position** drop-down menu, select: **Above selected item**.

6 Click on: **OK**.

You will see that the new caption is at the top of the image and the old caption is still at the bottom of the image. The number 1 after the new caption indicates that this is the first caption in the document.

You can change the format of the numbering by clicking on the numbering button in the Caption dialogue box. Have a look at the options when you apply the next caption.

5.9 Add a numbered caption to an image, figure, table or worksheet

Now you are going to add a caption to the NEW STOCK THIS WEEK table.

1   Select the table, i.e. **Table**: **Select**: **Table**.

2   Right-click to access the pop-up menu, then select: **Caption**. The Caption dialogue box appears. This offers you the next caption, i.e. **The Narrowboat Company 2**, as the caption.

3   Click on: **OK**. The caption is added to the table.

Now add a caption to the pie chart. This caption will be: **The Narrowboat Company 3**.

Method

1   Right-click on the pie chart to access the pop-up menu.

Handy Hint

Do not double-click to select the pie chart, because you will not get the pop-up menu you need.

2   Select: **Caption**. The Caption dialogue box appears offering you the caption.

3   Click on: **OK**.

On further thought, you don't need a caption for the NEW STOCK THIS WEEK table. Delete the caption by selecting and pressing the Delete key.

Update existing captions

Although you have deleted caption 2, the image (company logo) and the pie chart still have caption 1 and caption 3 attached to them. You need to update the captions.

Method

1   Select the caption text: **The Narrowboat Company 3**.

2   Right-click to access the pop-up menu, then select: **Update Field**. The caption should change to: The Narrowboat Company 2.

Handy Hint

You can amend or delete the captions by clicking into them on the page. However, if you delete the number your caption will not be included when you update. If you click the I-beam cursor just before the number, you will see that the number is in a grey field area.

Save your work as: **Task 5**.

Practice Task   *Task 5*

These exercises are included to help the candidate in his or her training for the Advanced ECDL program. The exercises included in this material are not Advanced ECDL certification tests and should not be construed in any way as Advanced ECDL certification tests. For information about Authorised ECDL Test Centres in different National Territories, please refer to the ECDL Foundation website at **www.ecdl.com**.

You have been asked to produce details of holidays lasting 7 and 8 nights.

1 Key in the following text for the 7-night holidays. Use the Tab key to move from column to column. Do not set up the text as a table. Do not put more than one tab between the columns.

```
7-night holidays¶
12·Apr–9·May→340¶
10·May–23·May    →     210¶
24·May–6·Jun→420¶
7·Jun–20·Jun →  360¶
21·Jun–·4·Jul → 398¶
5·Jul–18·Jul →  440¶
30·Aug–5·Sep→337¶
```

2 Convert the text to a table and AutoFit to contents. Do not include the table heading. (AM3.4.1.2)

Handy Hint

Separate text at tabs.

3 Create a column chart that shows the dates and the prices for 7-night holidays. (AM3.4.4.2)

4 Position the chart underneath the table. (AM3.4.4.4)

5 Make the following amendments:

- Change the colour of the background to yellow.
- Remove the gridlines.
- Change the chart to a bar chart. (AM3.4.4.3)

6 Insert an extra row at the top of the table to contain the column headings, and add a column to the right of '7 nights'. Key in the following details:

Dates	7 nights	Extra night (£)
12 Apr–9 May	340	18
10 May–23 May	210	21
24 May–6 Jun	420	28
7 Jun–20 Jun	360	34
21 Jun–4 Jul	398	39
5 Jul–18 Jul	440	44
30 Aug–5 Sep	337	26

7 Insert an extra column to the right of the 'Extra night' column.

- Insert the heading: 8 nights.
- Using a formula, calculate the cost of the 8-night holiday for each time period. (AM3.4.1.4)

Handy Hint

Each time, check that the formula is: =SUM(LEFT). If not, key in the correct formula.

8 Select the number format that gives you the £ symbol and the total to 2 decimal places.

9 Insert a row at the bottom of the table.

10 Using a formula, calculate the average cost of the 7-night holidays and the average cost of the 8-night holidays. (AM3.4.1.4)

Handy Hint

Look in: Paste function. The formula you need to create is =AVERAGE(ABOVE).

11 Select the number format that gives you the £ symbol and the total to 2 decimal places.

12 Sort the holidays into Ascending order of cost for 8 nights. (AM3.4.1.3)

Handy Hint

Select the rows you want to sort, otherwise Word includes the last row of the table in the sort.

13 Above the table, insert a picture that represents holidays.

14 Add the caption above the image: Holidays in the Sun. (AM3.4.6.2)

15 Amend the 7-nights price for 7 Jun–20 Jun to £460. Don't forget to update the Formula field in the 8-nights column. (AM3.3.2.2)

Handy Hint

Right-click in the cell containing the formula.

16 Update the chart with the new price by amending the datasheet. (AM3.4.4.3)

Handy Hint

Double-click on the chart to access the datasheet.

17 Save your work as: **Task 5 Answer**.

In this task, you will cover the following skills:

- Create new character and paragraph styles.
  - o The Style drop-down menu.
  - o Creating a new style.
  - o Applying a new style.
- Create a table of contents.
  - o Add page numbers to a document.
  - o Creating a table of contents.
- Apply formatting to a table of contents.
  - o Leader options.
  - o Add a heading to a table of contents.

- Update an existing table of contents.
  - o Remove existing contents.
  - o Add new contents.
- Use drawing options to create a simple drawing.
  - o Using the Drawing Toolbar.
  - o Create a basic drawing using AutoShapes.
  - o Group the elements of a drawing.
  - o Add colour to a drawing.
  - o Add 3-D effects to a drawing.

Scenario

*Open the file from the folder 'Task Files' called: **Task 6**. The file contains Robert Louis Stevenson's, A Child's Garden of Verses. The verses are already in numerical order, but to make it easier for the Literary Group members to go directly to the verse under discussion, a contents page would be useful.*

6.1 Create new character and paragraph styles

As you can see when you scroll through the document, it contains a variety of text fonts and sizes. In order to set up a table of contents, specific styles have to be applied to the text so that Word knows what to look for when setting up the contents page.

The Style drop-down menu

Styles can be used to format a number of sections of text that are not adjacent to each other, e.g. if you wanted all your subheadings in 16 pt, bold, italic, you could create the style and then for all the subsequent subheadings you simply select the style from the drop-down menu.

The Style drop-down menu is the first drop-down menu on the formatting toolbar. Click on this menu now and you will see that it already contains default styles.

Creating a new style

1 Click into the first verse title, i.e. 'Bed in Summer'.

2 Click on: **Format** from the main menu toolbar, then select: **Style**. The Style dialogue box appears.

3 Click on: **New**. The New Style dialogue box appears.

4 In the **Name** box, key in: **Verse Title**.

5 In the **Based on** box, select: **(no style)**. (You need to scroll to the top of the list of options.) No style is selected because the other option is to have your new style based on an existing style; this may not be exactly what you want.

Figure 6.1 Formatting text style using the New Style dialogue box

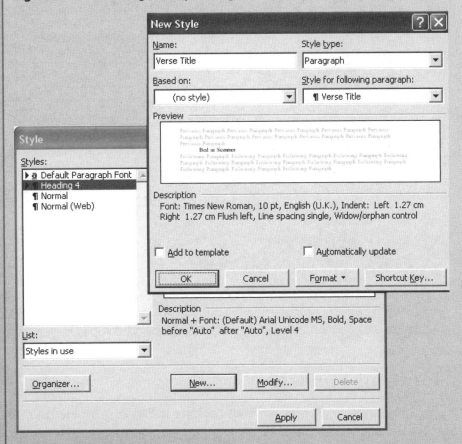

6 Click on the **Format** drop-down menu, then select: **Font**. The Font dialogue box appears.

7 Select the **Font** tab. Make your selections from this box, as follows:

   o **Font**: Snap ITC
   o **Font style**: Bold
   o **Size**: 16 pt
   o **Font color**: Red
   o **Effects**: Shadow

Figure 6.2 Selecting formatting options in the Font dialogue box

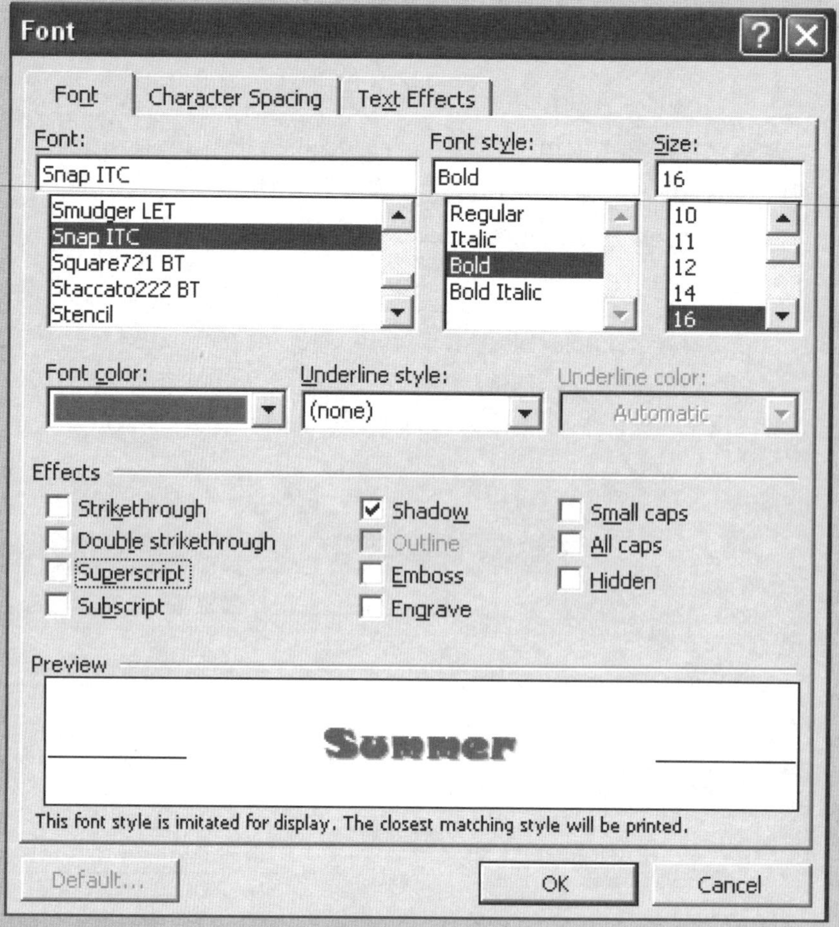

8 Click on: **OK** to exit the Font dialogue box, then click on: **OK** to exit the New Style dialogue box.

9 In the **Style** dialogue box, click on: **Apply**. This will exit the dialogue box. The first verse title should now appear in the new style.

Applying a new style

Check in the Style drop-down menu on the formatting toolbar that the new heading style you have created, i.e. Verse Title, appears in the list.

Method Click on: **Format**: **Style**, then from the list select: **Verse Title**. You can see in the Paragraph Preview and Character Preview windows the details of the Verse Title style.

Create new character and paragraph styles

Figure 6.3 Accessing a chosen style in the Style drop-down menu

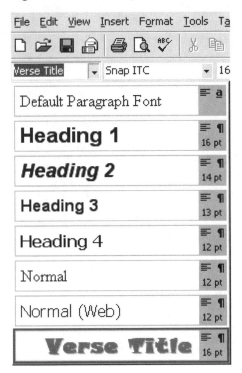

There is no quick way to do the next part. In the Word document, you need to click into each of the verse titles and then select your new style from the Style drop-down box. Continue until all the verse titles have the Verse Title style applied.

| **Handy Hint** | Beware! If you miss applying the Verse Title style to any of the verse titles, that title will not appear in your table of contents. |

6.2 Create a table of contents

A table of contents is a list created from formatted text that has a specified style applied to it. Typically a table of contents will be found at the front of the book, e.g. as a list of chapters and page numbers. Word picks up the style, in order, and lists the formatted text with the page on which it appears.

Add page numbers to a document

Before you create a table of contents (TOC), it is necessary to add page numbers to the document.

1 To insert page numbers at the bottom of the pages, select: **Insert**: **Page Numbers**. The Page Numbers dialogue box will appear.

2 Deselect the option: **Show number on first page**. (The first page is eventually going to be the front cover.)

3 Click on: **OK**.

Figure 6.4 Inserting page numbers using the Page Numbers dialogue box

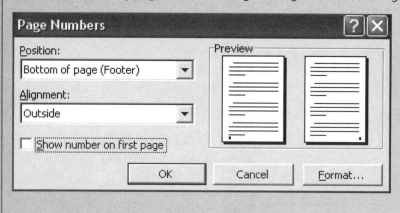

In the Page Numbers dialogue box, from the **Alignment** drop-down menu, choosing **Outside** will place the page numbers at the bottom of the pages alternating from left to right (even numbers on the right). This means that when a document is produced back to back, the page numbers will show on the outside edge of the booklet.

Creating a table of contents

You are now going to create a table of contents for *A Child's Garden of Verses*.

First, you need to create a space at the beginning of the document to accommodate the Contents page.

1 Position the I-beam cursor at the start of your document, i.e. before the number I. (Use the **Ctrl + Home** keys.)

2 Select: **Insert**: **Break** to access the **Break** dialogue box.

3 Click to select: **Page break**.

4 Click on: **OK**.

An alternative way to insert a page break is to hold down the **Ctrl** key and press **Enter**.

Method

1 Position the cursor at the top of the new page 1.

2 Click on: **Insert** from the main menu bar, then select: **Index and Tables**. An Index and Tables dialogue box appears.

3 Select the **Table of Contents** tab.

4 Click on the **Options** button at the bottom of the dialogue box. The Table of Contents Options dialogue box appears.

5 Scroll down to the bottom of the **TOC level** list; you should find Verse Title (see Figure 6.5).

6 As you only want one TOC level, i.e. all the verses listed underneath each other and left aligned, next to the Verse Title style, key in the number 1. A tick appears next to Verse Title.

Figure 6.5 Setting a table of contents using the TOC level

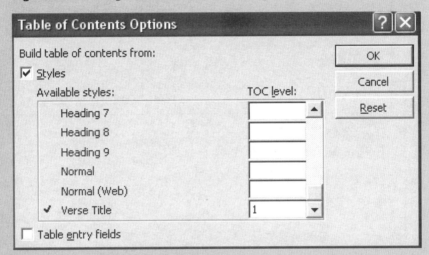

7 Click on: **OK** twice, to exit the two dialogues boxes. You should now have a table of contents on your first page.

The verse titles on the contents page are now linked to the verse titles in the main body of the document. Click on one of the titles; the cursor should go straight to that verse.

6.3 Apply formatting to a table of contents

Leader options

The contents page would be easier to follow if the leader dots were a solid line.

1 Press: **Ctrl + Home** to take you to the top of the contents page without accidentally clicking in the table of contents and ending up even further down the document. This method also selects the table of contents, which you need to do before altering the leader dots.

2 Click on: **Insert** from the main menu toolbar, then select: **Index** and **Tables**.

3 In the **Index and Tables** dialogue box, select the **Table of Contents** tab.

4 From the **Tab leader** drop-down menu, select the **solid line** option.

Figure 6.6 Using Tab leader in the Index and Tables dialogue box

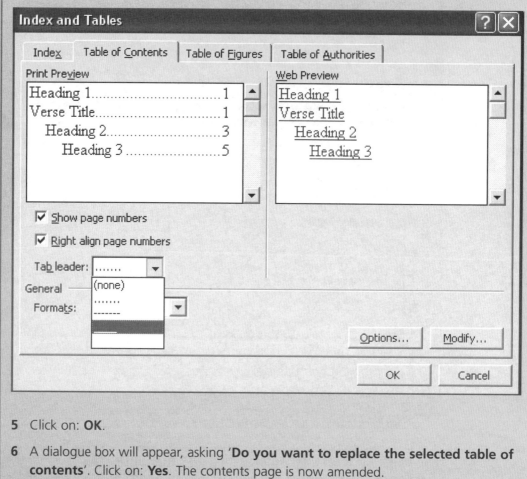

5 Click on: **OK**.

6 A dialogue box will appear, asking '**Do you want to replace the selected table of contents**'. Click on: **Yes**. The contents page is now amended.

Add a heading to a table of contents

To finish the page, you can add the heading 'Contents' above the table of contents.

1 Use the **Ctrl + Home** keys to get to the top of the page.

2 Press: **Enter** twice to create two line spaces.

3 Key in the word: **Contents**.

4 Increase the character spacing of the word Contents, as follows:

   o Click on: **Format**: **Font**.
   o In the Font dialogue box, select the **Character Spacing** tab.

- In the **Scale** box, change the per cent to: **300**. (300 is not listed in the drop-down menu, so you will need to key '300' in the scale box.)
- Click on: **OK**.

Figure 6.7 Formatting a heading on the Character Spacing tab in the Font dialogue box

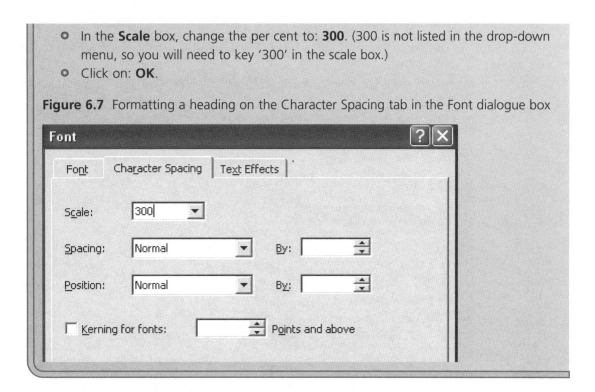

Update an existing table of contents

6.4

Remove existing contents

Apart from the time it saves creating one manually, one of the greatest advantages of setting up a table of contents automatically is that if you decide that you don't want to include, for example, a certain verse, then you can delete it from your document and update the table of contents.

Method

1 Select and delete: **Verse XIV**: **Where go the boats?** You can get quickly to this verse by clicking on the title in the table of contents.

Figure 6.8 Select and delete the chosen verse

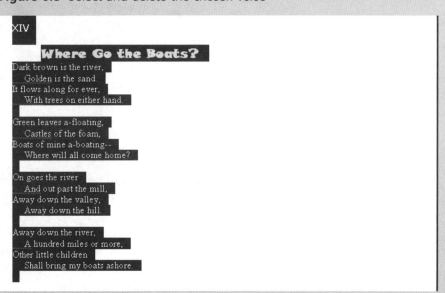

2 Right-click on your first page (the table of contents). The table of contents is now shaded and a pop-up menu has appeared.

3 From the pop-up menu, select: **Update Field**.

Figure 6.9 From the pop-up menu, select: Update Field

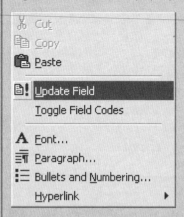

4 An **Update Table of Contents** dialogue box appears. You will be asked which part of the table of contents you want to update: either **Update page numbering** only or **Update entire table**. As you have changed more than the page number, i.e. you have deleted part of the document, select: **Update entire table**.

Figure 6.10 Selecting a chosen update option in the Update Table of Contents dialogue box

5 Click on: **OK**.

6 Save your work as: **Task 6**.

The contents page should now reflect the changes, i.e. 'Where go the boats?' is no longer listed in the table of contents.

Add new contents

The above method can also be used to include new verse. Remember to apply the relevant style to the text you want included in the table of contents.

Use the drawing options to create a simple drawing

Create a front cover

Open the **Task 6** document (if it isn't open already). Go to the top of the document (**Ctrl + Home** keys). The document needs a front cover now. To create a new first page, insert a page break in front of the contents page (press **Ctrl + Enter**).

Handy Hint

Don't forget to update your table of contents. All the verses will now be on different page numbers.

You are going to create a simple boat for the front cover. Figure 6.11 is an example of what your finished work may look like.

Figure 6.11 The boat for the front cover will look something like this

Creating a drawing that is going to fill the whole page is easier to do if you can see the whole page you are working on.

Method

Click on: **Zoom** from the standard toolbar and select: **Whole Page**.

Figure 6.12 Click on Zoom: Whole Page to view the whole page you are working on

Help

500%		
200%		
150%		
100%		
75%		
50%		
25%		
10%		
Page Width		
Text Width		
Whole Page		
Two Pages		

Using the Drawing Toolbar

To create the drawing, you will be using tools from the Drawing Toolbar only. Make sure that you have this toolbar visible at the foot of the screen. If not:

Method

Click on: **View**: **Toolbars**: **Drawing**. The Drawing Toolbar is positioned at the bottom of your screen.

Figure 6.13 The Drawing Toolbar

Handy Hint

Caution: the following instructions assume that you click and drag from top left to bottom right.

Create a basic drawing using AutoShapes

The first shape is going to be the hull of the boat.

Method

1 Click on the **AutoShapes** drop-down menu, then select: **Basic Shapes**. Select the third option on the top row: **Trapezoid**.

2 Click on the page at approximately 16 cm on the vertical ruler. Drag the black cross across the page until you get a basic 'hull' shape (see Figure 6.14).

Figure 6.14 Using the Trapezoid AutoShape to create the boat hull

Click down here

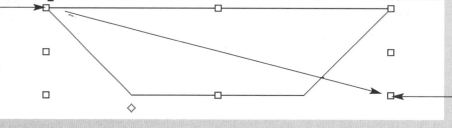

Drag diagonally to here

3 For the mast, select the **Line** tool which is located to the right of AutoShapes. Click on a central point along the top of the hull and drag upwards until you get a vertical line that represents a mast.

Handy Hint

Keep referring back to the finished illustration (Figure 6.11 on page 87).

4 For the sails, from the **AutoShapes** drop-down menu, select: **Basic Shapes**, then select the fourth option on the second row: **Right Triangle**. Click near the top of the mast (leave room for a flag) and drag right to form the right-hand sail.

Handy Hint

If you don't like your first effort, it is easier to adjust the shape using the handles than to try again.

5 For the sail on the opposite side, select the same Right Triangle AutoShape. For the left-hand sail, you need to flip it. Draw the triangle first, then from the **Draw** drop-down menu, select: **Rotate or Flip**: **Flip Horizontal**.

Use the drawing options to create a simple drawing

Figure 6.15 To flip the sail, from the Draw drop-down menu, select: Rotate or Flip: Flip Horizontal

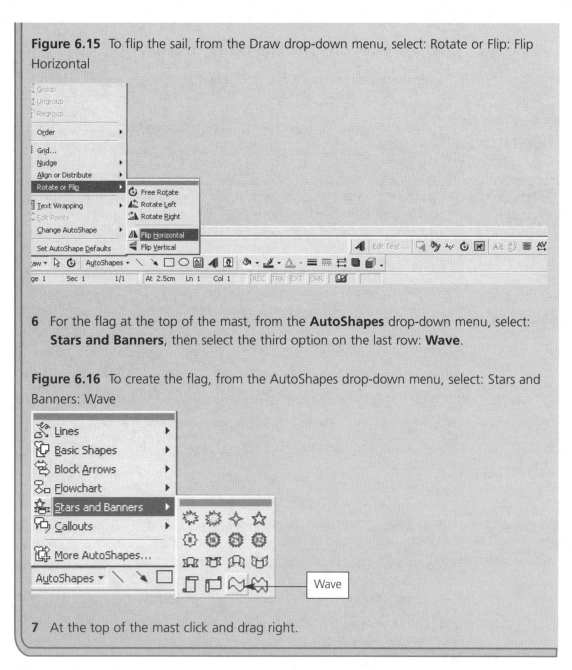

6   For the flag at the top of the mast, from the **AutoShapes** drop-down menu, select: **Stars and Banners**, then select the third option on the last row: **Wave**.

Figure 6.16 To create the flag, from the AutoShapes drop-down menu, select: Stars and Banners: Wave

7   At the top of the mast click and drag right.

You should now have a simple line drawing of a sailing boat that looks approximately like Figure 6.17.

Figure 6.17 The sailing boat shape should look like this

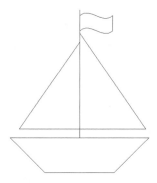

If the size and/or shapes are not quite right and you want to adjust them, click on the shape you want to adjust and resize by dragging the handles.

Group the elements of a drawing

To keep all the elements of the boat together, you can group them.

1 On the Drawing Toolbar, click on: **Select Objects** (the white pointer tool), then draw a large box around all the parts of the boat.

You are really drawing a box around the handles, not the shapes that you can see on-screen, so make sure that your box is big enough.

Figure 6.18 Group the elements of the drawing using Select Objects

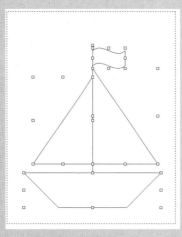

This method is faster than holding down the Shift key and selecting each AutoShape individually.

You should now have all the AutoShapes selected. If not, try again but draw a larger box to make sure that you pick up all the handles.

2 Click on: **Draw**, then select: **Group**. One box and one set of handles will appear around the boat.

If you click anywhere in the boat and drag the drawing, the whole boat should move.

To include the sea in the picture:

1 From the **AutoShapes** drop-down menu, select: **Stars and Banners**, then select the last option on the last row: **Double Wave**.

2 Click at the point where you want the waterline to be and drag from the left-hand side of the page to the bottom right-hand corner.

Figure 6.19 To create the sea, select: AutoShapes: Stars and Banners: Wave

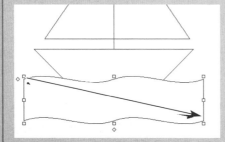

Use the drawing options to create a simple drawing

To put the wavy text inside the 'sea':

1   Click on the **Insert WordArt** icon  .

2   Select the blue wave text from the fourth row.

3   Click on: **OK**.

4   Key in: **Poetry for Children**.

Figure 6.20 In WordArt, key in: Poetry for Children

The text will appear on the screen. Click and drag the WordArt into position in the sea. Drag out the corner handles to resize.

Dragging with the corner handles maintains the original proportion of the WordArt.

To create the sun:

From the AutoShapes drop-down menu, select: **Basic Shapes**: **Sun**.

To keep the image circular, hold down the **Shift** key when you drag out the drawing.

Add colour to a drawing

You can now add colour to your picture. You are going to use the **Fill Color** icon , the **Line Color** icon and the **Font Color** icon **A** from the Drawing

Toolbar. Run the I-beam cursor over these icons at the bottom of your screen, to see the icon labels.

Method

Click on the document in the **Sun AutoShape**. From the **Fill Color** pop-up menu, select: **Yellow**. (To access the pop-up menu, you will need to click on the down arrow next to the icon.)

Before you can repeat this process for the rest of the picture, you will need to ungroup the boat AutoShapes.

Method

Right-click on the drawing to access the pop-up menu, then select: **Grouping**: **Ungroup**.

Don't forget to use more Fill Colors and Fill Effects. For the sea:

Method

1 Select: **Fill Color**: **Dark Blue**, then select: **Fill Effects**.

2 In the **Fill Effects** dialogue box, select the **Gradient** tab, then select: **Horizontal**.

3 Using the **Dark to Light** scroll bar, change the density of the colour.

Figure 6.21 In Fill Effects, change the destiny of colour using the Dark to Light scrollbar

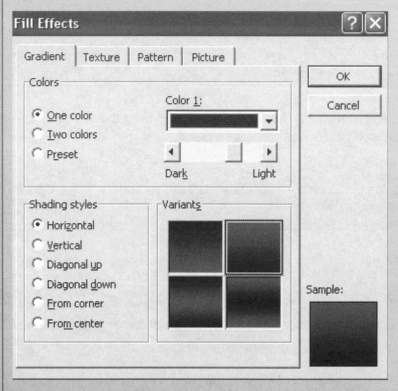

4 Once you are happy with the boat, **Group** the whole page.

5 Save your work.

Use the drawing options to create a simple drawing

Add 3-D effects to a drawing

To add 3-D effects to the drawing:

Method

1 Click on the drawing.

2 From the Drawing Toolbar, select the **3-D Style** icon  .

3 Experiment by clicking on the different effects. If you don't like your choices, click on the Undo button to go back. You can get even more effects from the **3D-Settings** menu.

Figure 6.22 The 3-D Settings menu

When you have made your final selection(s), save your work as **Task 6**. Click on the **Print Preview** icon then select: **Multiple Pages** to view your work. You will see that you have completed a substantial piece of work of approximately 23 pages.

Practice Task | *Task 6*

These exercises are included to help the candidate in his or her training for the Advanced ECDL program. The exercises included in this material are not Advanced ECDL certification tests and should not be construed in any way as Advanced ECDL certification tests. For information about Authorised ECDL Test Centres in different National Territories, please refer to the ECDL Foundation website at **www.ecdl.com**.

Method

You are going to set up a document that contains a selection of Aesop's fables. The document will have a front cover and a table of contents at the end. The main body text of the fables is to be input by an operator at a later date.

1 From the Task Files folder, open the file: **Aesops Fables**.

> The bat and the weasels
>
> A bat who fell upon the ground and was caught by a weasel pleaded to be spared his life. The weasel refused, saying …
>
> The ass and the grasshopper
>
> An ass having heard some grasshoppers chirping, was highly enchanted; and, desiring to possess them …
>
> The lion and the mouse
>
> A lion was awakened from sleep by a mouse running over his face. Rising up angrily, he caught him and was about to kill him, when …
>
> The boy hunting locusts

A boy was hunting for locusts. He had caught a goodly number, when he saw a scorpion, and mistaking him for a locust, reached out …

The mole and his mother

A mole, a creature blind from birth, once said to his mother: 'I am sure that I can see, mother!' In the desire to prove to him his mistake, his …

The traveller and his dog

A traveller about to set out on a journey saw his dog stand at the door stretching himself. He asked him sharply: 'Why do you stand …

Hercules and the wagoner

A carter was driving a wagon along a country lane, when the wheels sank down deep into a rut. The rustic driver, stupefied and aghast …

The bear and the fox

A bear boasted very much of his philanthropy, saying that of all animals he was the most tender in his regard for man, for he had such …

The dog in the manger

A dog lay in a manger, and by his growling and snapping prevented the oxen from eating the hay which had been placed …

2 Save your work as: **Task 6 Answer**.

3 Apply a password to the document to:

   ○ Protect your work (use your first name)
   ○ Modify your work (use your surname). This password will allow the operator access to your work.

4 Create a style for the subheadings:

   ○ Choose any font or colour.
   ○ Choose a 16–20 font size.
   ○ Ensure that you give your style a name that is easily identifiable in the Style drop-down menu. (AM3.1.2.4)

   (The suggested answer has been created in Papyrus 18 pt font.)

5 Create a style for the body text of the fables. Choose a font smaller than the subheadings.

   (The suggested answer has been created in Lucida Bright, 12 pt font.)

6 Format Paragraph to 1.5 line spacing with a first line indent.

7 Apply the new styles to the text by selecting them from the Style drop-down menu.

8 Create a blank page 1.

Handy Hint

Insert a page break at the top of the first page.

9 Insert page numbers at the top of the page. Apply lower case Roman numerals and centre. Do not show page numbers on the first page.

10 Create a table of contents to start on a new page after the last fable. (AM3.2.2.1). Apply a classic or distinctive format, with page numbers and dotted tab leaders. (AM3.2.2.3)

The fables will appear on page 2 or 3 until the remainder of the fables are keyed in and the table of contents has been updated.

11 Key in the following fable at the top of page 2.

The Stag, The Wolf, And The Sheep

A STAG asked a sheep to lend him a measure of wheat, and said that the wolf would be his surety. The sheep, fearing some fraud …

12 Update the table of contents. (AM3.2.2.2)

To create the front page you are going to use the drawing tools.

13 Create an abstract picture using AutoShapes. (See a finished example in the answers section.) (AM3.4.5.2)

14 Use WordArt to insert the title: Aesop's Fables.

15 Apply Fill, Order and Rotate to the AutoShapes.

16 Group the AutoShapes wherever possible.

17 Print 4 pages per sheet. (AM3.6.1.4)

18 Save your work.

Letters to speakers

In this task, you will cover the following skills:

- Create a new template.
- Change formatting and layout of a template.
  - Insert a date field.
  - Save a new template.
- Edit a mail merge data source and data file.
  - Amend a data file.
  - Produce a form letter.
  - Using merge fields.
- Apply automatic text formatting.
  - Amend AutoText options.
  - Apply letter case options in AutoCorrect.
- Merge a document with a data source or data file using certain criteria.
  - Access a data file using Mail Merge.
  - Make selections from a data file.
- Sort data source or data file records.
- Record a basic macro.
  - Assign a keyboard shortcut to a macro.

- Recording the macro.
- Assigning a toolbar shortcut to a macro.
- Run a macro.
  - Run a macro using a keyboard shortcut.
  - Run a macro assigned to a toolbar.
- Assign a macro button to a toolbar or create a macro toolbar.
  - Add a macro button to an existing toolbar.
  - Create a macro toolbar.
- Copy a macro.
- Amend or update field code entries.
  - Remove Form Field options.
  - Update date and time manually.
- Use AutoText.
- Use check boxes.
- Delete items in a form.

Scenario

The Literary Discussion Group would like to send out letters to their regular speakers, to invite them to put forward topics for the next round of meetings. They have provided a file with the names of the speakers, their addresses and their favourite venues. They would like a system setting up so that they can use their file to pick out the most appropriate people for the venue. This will involve producing a merged document (the finished letters) using the data from the supplied file and a form letter (a standard letter).

7.1 Create a new template

A letter heading for the Literary Discussion Group has not been provided. This means that you will need to create a template that can be used each time the Literary Discussion Group wants to send out letters.

Microsoft Office has a selection of templates for users to amend according to their own available specifications. You access these from the **File** menu on the main menu toolbar.

Method

1 Click on: **File**: **New**. The New dialogue box appears.

2 Select the **Letters & Faxes** tab, then select: **Contemporary Letter**.

3 In the **Create New** box, click on the **Template** radio button.

Figure 7.1 Creating a new template in File: New

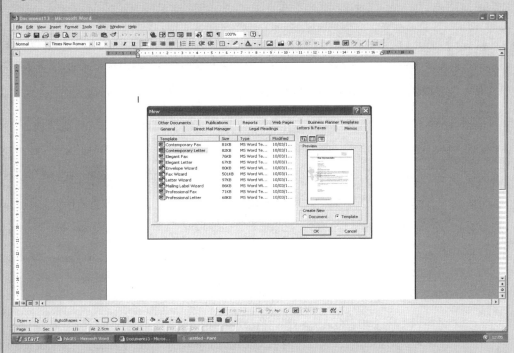

4 Click on: **OK**. The template to be amended appears on screen.

5 Click in the top right-hand corner box where the words **Click here and type return address** appear.

6 Key in the address of the Literary Discussion Group (see Figure 7.2). Change the font size to 12 pt.

7 Triple-click on: **Company name here**. Insert: **Literary Discussion Group**.

Figure 7.2 Key in the Literary Discussion Group details on the template

45 High Street
BRADFORD
Yorkshire
YY1 8PB

Literary Discussion Group

Next, the date needs to go onto the template. The date needs to update each time the template is opened. There is already a date field underneath the shaded bar, but it is not in the format you would like and it needs removing.

Method | To remove the field, highlight with the I-beam cursor to select, then press the **Delete** key.

Insert a date field

To insert the date:

Method

1 Click on: **Insert** from the main menu bar, then select: **Date and Time**.

2 Select the third option: **XX month XXXX**.

3 Select the **Update Automatically** box.

4 Click on: **OK**.

The date should now be on the template.

The rest of the text on the template is not appropriate for the Literary Discussion Group's needs. Select the text and delete. There is also a 'slogan' box at the bottom of the document. Delete this too.

Save a new template

To save your new template:

Method

1 Select: **File**: **Save As**. The Save As dialogue box appears.

Figure 7.3 The Save As dialogue box

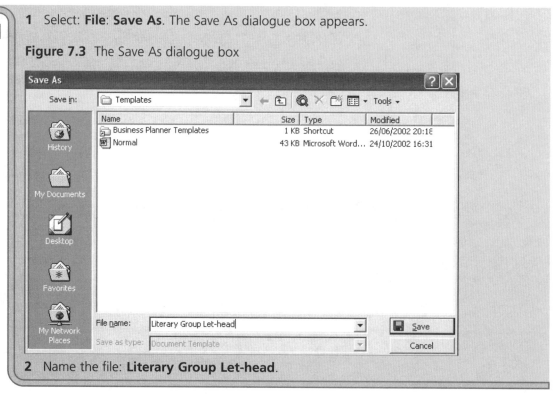

2 Name the file: **Literary Group Let-head**.

In the **Save as type** box, you will see that you cannot access **Document Template**. One of the effects of saving as a template is that the software puts the extension **.dot** at the end of the file name, rather than **.doc** (as it does for documents); this saves the file to a **Template** folder.

The Literary Group Let-head file will open as a template (.dot), but you will be able to save it as a document (.doc). The original template will remain unchanged.

Figure 7.4 The new template appears in the General tab in File: New

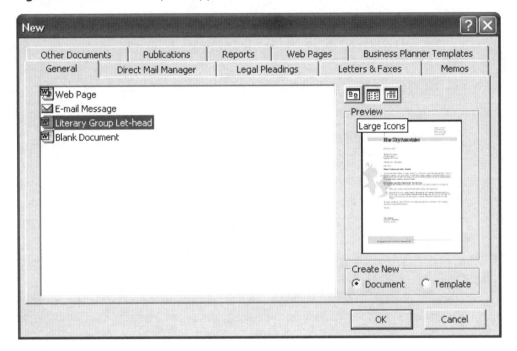

7.3 Edit a mail merge data source and data file

Amend a data file

Before you can produce the letters, you need to make some amendments to the data file that you have received from the group.

Mrs Lynn Westerly
98 Wharfe Road
Barnoldswick
Lancs
BB3 2RJ
Kenwood Hall

One of the records needs to be deleted. Julie Platt is entered twice: once as Ms and once as Mrs. Julie would like to be addressed as Mrs. To delete the unwanted record:

Method

1   Click anywhere on the line to be deleted.

2   Select: **Table** from the main menu toolbar, then select: **Delete**: **Rows**. The row will disappear.

Handy Hint

You must use this method: if you simply highlight the text and press the delete key, you will remove the words but not the row, i.e. you will be left with blank cells as shown in Figure 7.5.

Figure 7.5 You will be left with a blank row if you highlight the text and press the delete key

Mrs	Julie	Platt	56 Cross Avenue	Nelson	Lancs	BB9 1DR	Earby Library Room
Mr	Steven	Mossley	89 Booth Avenue	Rastrick	Yorks	YO3 4TB	Earby Library Room

3   Save the file using the same name.

Produce a form letter

Using the Literary Let-head Template, you are going to produce the form letter. This is the document that will combine (merge) with the data file containing the names of the speakers. The reason for using a data file and a form letter is that you can use the two over and over again, making different selections from the data file each time.

Method

1   Open the Literary Let-head Template on-screen. Leave at least one clear line space below the date.

2   Click on: **Tools**: **Mailmerge**. The **Mail Merge Helper** dialogue box appears.

3   From the **Create** drop-down menu, select: **Form Letters**.

4   From the **Edit** drop-down menu, select: **Active Window** (because you are going to use the file on-screen as the form letter).

5   From the **Get Data** drop-down menu, select: **Open Data Source**.

Edit a mail merge data source and data file

Figure 7.6 Selecting form letter options in Mail Merge Helper dialogue box

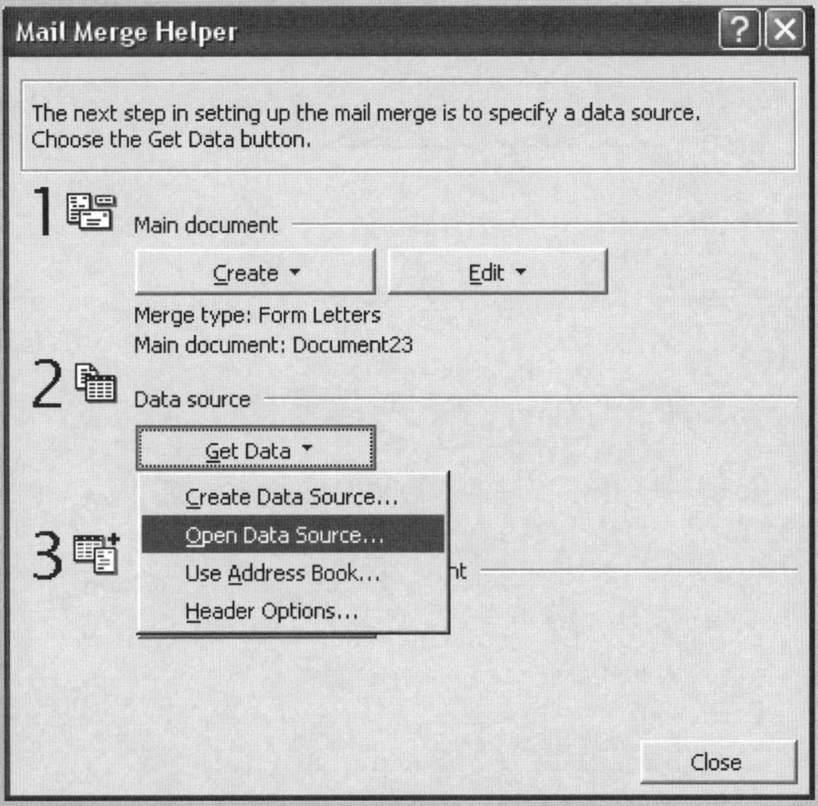

Mail Merge Helper

The next step in setting up the mail merge is to specify a data source.
Choose the Get Data button.

1 Main document

Create ▾   Edit ▾

Merge type: Form Letters
Main document: Document23

2 Data source

Get Data ▾

Create Data Source...
Open Data Source...
Use Address Book...
Header Options...

3

Close

6 Select the file: **Mail Merge Data** that you amended and click on: **Open**.

7 Click on: **Edit Main Document**.

The **Mail Merge Toolbar** should have appeared underneath the Formatting Toolbar.

As you worked through the above sequence, you will have noticed that you had more than one option from which to choose. Although this process seems complicated at first, it becomes clearer with practice. In reality, it is easy to make the correct choices as you would know what information and files you are working with.

Using merge fields

You are now going to build up the name and address for the letter using Merge Fields, and key in the body of the letter.

Method

1 Click down underneath the date, leaving a clear line space.

2 On the **Mail Merge Toolbar**, click on: **Insert Merge Field**. You should see a drop-down list that corresponds with the headings in the data file.

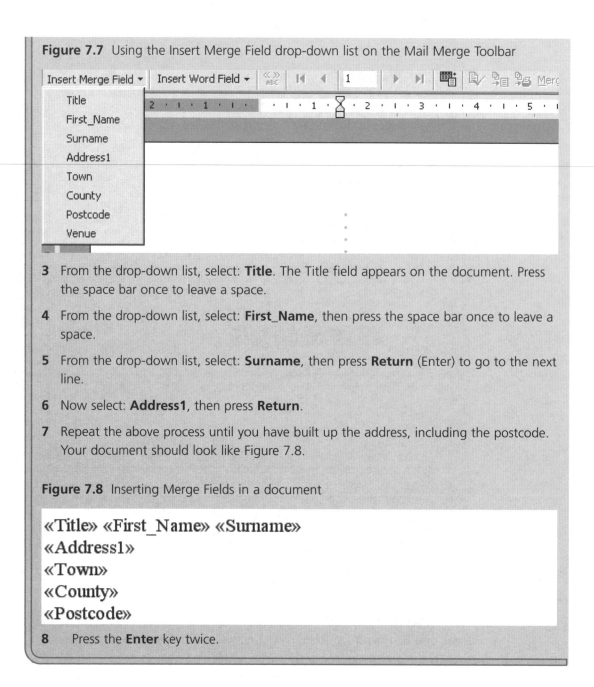

Figure 7.7 Using the Insert Merge Field drop-down list on the Mail Merge Toolbar

3 From the drop-down list, select: **Title**. The Title field appears on the document. Press the space bar once to leave a space.

4 From the drop-down list, select: **First_Name**, then press the space bar once to leave a space.

5 From the drop-down list, select: **Surname**, then press **Return** (Enter) to go to the next line.

6 Now select: **Address1**, then press **Return**.

7 Repeat the above process until you have built up the address, including the postcode. Your document should look like Figure 7.8.

Figure 7.8 Inserting Merge Fields in a document

«Title» «First_Name» «Surname»
«Address1»
«Town»
«County»
«Postcode»

8 Press the **Enter** key twice.

7.4 Apply automatic text formatting

Amend AutoText options

Before you start to enter the text for the letter, this would be an appropriate time to look at the settings that you can apply so that Word automatically formats your text.

Method

1 Click on: **Format**, then select: **AutoFormat**. The AutoFormat dialogue box appears.

2 Click on: **Options**. An **AutoCorrect** dialogue box appears.

3 Click on the **AutoText** tab to see the default list of AutoText entries. You may have seen these in action: when you type 'Yours' at the end of a letter, you are offered the word 'truly' as the next word.

4 Scroll down the list and you will find 'Yours truly' is the last entry. To remove this, select: **Yours truly** from the list and click on: **Delete**.

Similarly, in the AutoCorrect dialogue box you can add your own AutoText:

Method

1   In the **Enter AutoText entries here** box, add the AutoText entry: **Yours sincerely**.

2   Click on: **Add**.

3   Click on: **OK**.

You will see that you are now offered this AutoText option at the end of the letter when you type the word 'Yours'.

Apply letter case options in AutoCorrect

If you produce documents that contain listed items on separate lines, you may wish to stop Word automatically inserting a capital letter at the start of each listed item. Apply this setting to your machine.

Method

1   In the **AutoCorrect** dialogue box, click on the **AutoCorrect tab**.

2   Click to deselect: **Capitalize first letter of sentences**.

3   Click on: **OK** twice to exit the dialogue boxes and to apply the AutoText and AutoCorrect settings.

4   Now key in the following letter (Figure 7.9), inserting the Merge Fields as you go along.

Figure 7.9 Insert Merge Fields while entering text into a Form Template

Dear «First_Name»

The next round of meetings is now being planned for «County». As you very kindly volunteered to give a talk on a topic of your own choice I would be grateful if you would forward your ideas to me so that I can check that you are not going to clash with another speaker.

We omitted to make this check last year and it proved very embarrassing for everyone concerned. Once again let me thank you for your very kind offer and I look forward to meeting you again on the evening.

Yours sincerely

Peter Smithson
Secretary

5   Now save this file as a document. Save as: **Form Letter**.

(Note: you may need to change the folder from Templates.)

Merge a document with a data source or data file using certain criteria

Access a data file using Mail Merge

You are about to bring together the information you want from the data file, i.e. all the speakers for Yorkshire, and sort the letters into order of surname.

Method

1 Click on the **Mail Merge Helper** icon (see Figure 7.10), or select: **Tools**: **Mail Merge**.

Figure 7.10 The Mail Merge Helper icon

Mail Merge Helper

2 The Mail Merge Helper dialogue box appears. You can see which files you have chosen as your **Main document** and your **Data source**. If you want to make any changes to the data file or the form letter, you can do so at this point, for example, if you had not used the files for some time and they needed updating or the letter needed changing slightly.

3 Under **Data source**, click on the **Edit** drop-down button, then select: **Data File**. The Data Form dialogue box appears. You can use the Data Form dialogue box to add new records, delete old records and, if you were handling a large database, find specific records.

Figure 7.11 The Data Form dialogue box

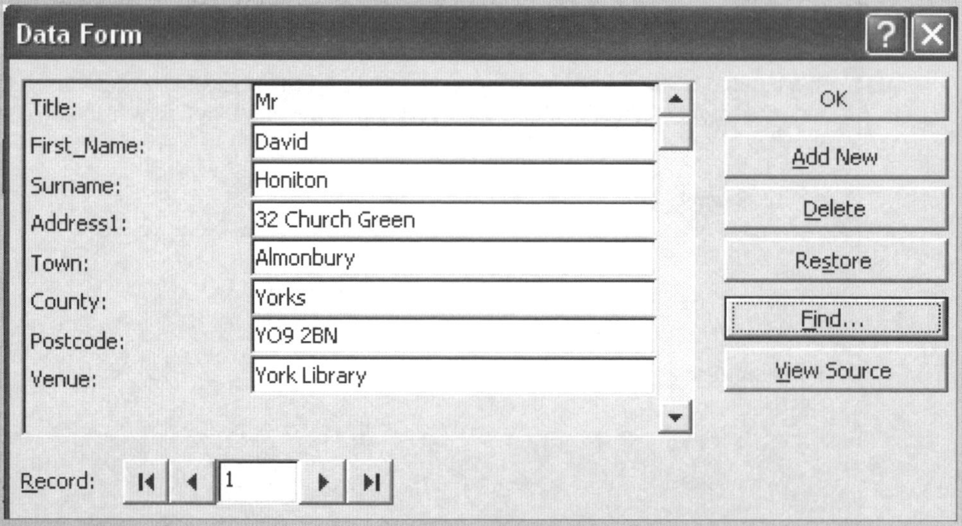

4 Click on: **OK** to exit the Data Form dialogue box.

Make selections from a data file

The next part is to filter out (select) the speakers from Yorkshire.

1 Click on the **Mail Merge Helper** icon, to access the Mail Merge Helper dialogue box.

2 Click on: **Query Options**.

3 Click on the **Filter Records** tab.

4 In the **Field** box, select: **County**.

5 In the **Comparison** box, select: **Equal to**.

6 In the **Compare to** box, type in: **Yorks**. Caution: do <u>not</u> click on: OK – you are going to sort the records first.

Figure 7.12 Selecting chosen data using the Filter Records tab in Query Options

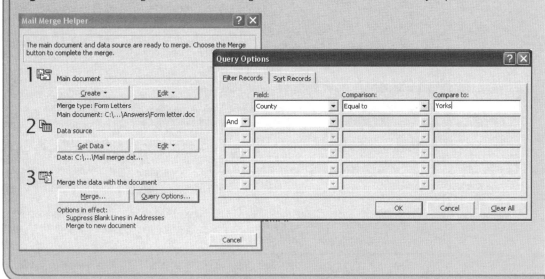

7.6 *Sort data source or data file records*

There are two ways you could sort the records into a specific order.

● You can do it before you use the Mail Merge Helper, i.e. when you have the data file on-screen. To use this method, you simply click in the table, then click on: Table: Sort, then make the selection(s) in the Sort dialogue box before clicking on: OK.

● The second and the most practical method, because it does not affect the original data file, is to sort the records using the Mail Merge Helper. Another benefit of this method is that, as you are already using the Mail Merge Helper, it is only one extra step.

Method

1 In the **Query Options** box, click on the **Sort Records** tab.

2 In **Sort by**, select: **Surname**.

Figure 7.13 Sort data records using the Sort Records tab in Query Options

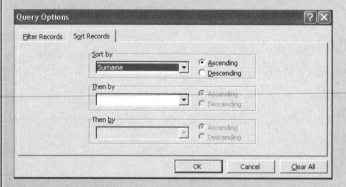

3 Click on: **OK**.

4 The Merge dialogue box now appears. Click on: **Merge**.

Figure 7.14 The Merge dialogue box

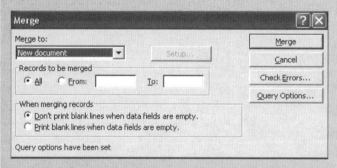

5 In the **Mail Merge Helper** dialogue box, click on: **Merge**.

6 You should now have a set of letters addressed to the speakers in Yorkshire. Save this file as: **Merged Letters**.

7 Check your letters. If you have any fields that have not picked up data, e.g. the County field, go back to your Form Letter (see page 103) and click on the Mail Merge Helper – you may have keyed in the entry incorrectly.

Handy Hint

Once you have merged your letters, you cannot Undo.

Now select the speakers from Lancashire.

Method

1 Using **File**: **Open**, return to the form letter. Click on the **Mail Merge Helper** icon.

2 In the **Mail Merge Helper** dialogue box, select: **Query Option**.

3 Select the **Filter Records** tab. In the **Compare to** box, key in: **Lancs**.

4 Click on: **OK**.

5 Click on: **Merge** to return to the Mail Merge Helper dialogue box.

6 Click on: **Merge**.

You will have a new set of letters addressed to speakers in Lancashire. You now have two sets of letters: one for speakers in Lancashire; one for speakers in Yorkshire.

Record a basic macro

Assign a keyboard shortcut to a macro

A macro is a function for saving (recording) a set of several formats that can be used over and over again. It saves time because you don't have to go through the separate (micro) changes each time you start a new document. You can also apply macros to existing documents.

At the beginning of the book, you performed many different formatting functions. These could have been recorded in a macro, ready for you to apply (run).

Method

1 From your folder **Task Files**, open the original file: **Text for Task 1**.

2 Select all the text (**Ctrl + A**).

3 Click on: **Tools**: **Macro**: **Record New Macro**.

Figure 7.15 Click on: Tools: Macro: Record New Macro

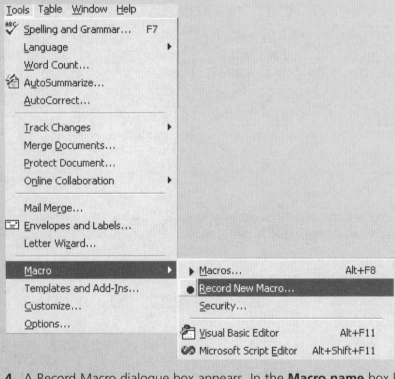

4 A Record Macro dialogue box appears. In the **Macro name** box key in: **LDG_BODY_TEXT**.

Handy Hint

If you want spaces between your words, you need to key in an underscore rather than using the spacebar.

5 In the **Store macro in** box, you will see that Word automatically defaults to saving as: **All Documents (Normal.dot)**.

Handy Hint

To save the macro in this document only: click on the **Store macro in** drop-down menu and select the name of the file, i.e. **Text for Task 1 (document)**. The macro will then be unavailable for other documents.

6 In the **Assign macro to** box, click to select: **Keyboard**.

Figure 7.16 Using the Record Macro dialogue box

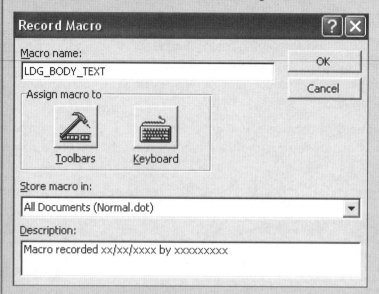

7 A **Customize Keyboard** dialogue box now appears (see Figure 7.17).

In the **Press new shortcut key** box, you have to assign a key. Most of the keys are already assigned: if you use a shortcut that is already assigned it will appear underneath the box. You can use an assigned shortcut if you wish, but it will override the original. Be careful that you don't override a shortcut that you use to format text, e.g. **Ctrl + B** for bold.

Ctrl + . (full-stop key) is not usually assigned, so for this exercise use **Ctrl + .** as the shortcut. Hold down the **Ctrl** key and press the **full-stop** key. Word automatically inserts the + symbol.

Figure 7.17 Creating a shortcut in Customize Keyboard

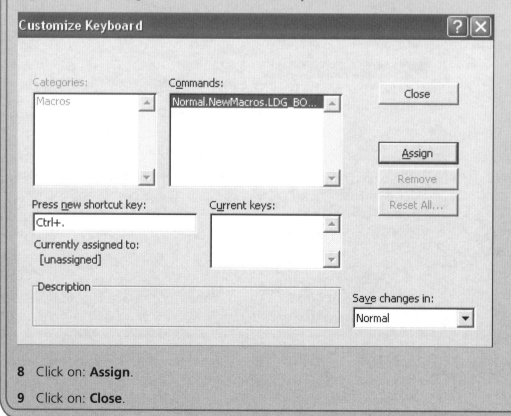

8 Click on: **Assign**.

9 Click on: **Close**.

If you do not click on Assign, the macro will not work.

The **Stop Recording** box now appears on-screen and an image of a cassette is attached to the pointer tool.

Figure 7.18 The Stop box

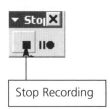

Stop Recording

Recording the macro

Don't panic at this stage: the process is not time-bound, i.e. you don't have to rush. You can only work on one section of selected text at a time, then you have to press stop and repeat the process for further sections of the text. For this example, you are going to record two macros.

If you make a mistake just press the stop button and start again. You will be asked if you want to replace the existing macro; click on: **Yes**.

Method

1 Click on: **Format**: **Columns**.

2 In the **Columns** dialogue box, make the following selections:

  o Number of columns: **2**
  o Click to select: **Line between**
  o Width: **7 cm**
  o Spacing: **4 cm** (you may need to deselect the Equal column width box).

3 Click on: **OK**.

4 Click on: **Format**: **Borders and Shading**.

5 In the **Borders and Shading** dialogue box, select the **Page Border** tab.

6 Make the following selections:

  o Setting: **Box**
  o Color: **Green**

7 Click on: **OK**.

8 On the Formatting Toolbar, click on the **Justify** icon.

9 Click on the **Stop recording** button.

The macro is now recorded and stored for further use.

Assigning a toolbar shortcut to a macro

To set up the next macro:

Method

1 Triple-click to select Paragraph 1.

2 From **Tools** on the main menu toolbar, select: **Macro**: **Record New Macro**.

3 In the **Record Macro** dialogue box, in the **Macro name** box key in: LDG_FIRST_PARA.

This time we are going to use the toolbar rather than a keyboard shortcut.

4 In the **Assign macro to** box, click to select: **Toolbars**.

5 The **Customize** dialogue box appears. You last used the Customize dialogue box at the start of the book to set the toolbars on a separate row using the Options tab. Now you will use the **Commands** tab.

Figure 7.19 The Customize dialogue box

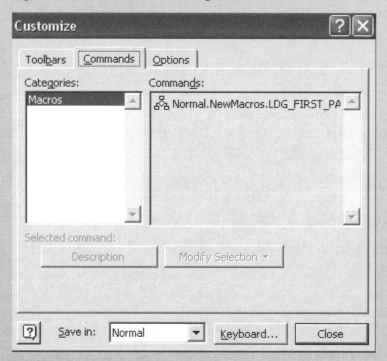

6 Click on: **Close**. The Stop Recording box and the cassette pointer tool now appear on-screen.

7 Click on: **Format**: **Borders and Shading**. The Borders and Shading dialogue box appears.

8 Click on the **Borders** tab, then select the following options:

- Setting: **Box**
- Color: **Automatic**
- Apply to: **Paragraph**

9 Click on the **Shading** tab, then select: **25% gray**.

10 Click on: **OK**.

11 Click on the **Stop recording** button.

You have now set up two macros. Close the file without saving. You will not lose the macros as they are saved to Normal.doc and are available to use on any document.

7.8 Run a macro

From your **Task Files** folder, open the **Text for Task 1** file. You are now going to run the macros you have recorded.

Run a macro using a keyboard shortcut

You are going to run the macro that was set up with the keyboard shortcut Ctrl + . (full-stop).

Method

Click in the text. Hold down the **Ctrl** key, then press the **full-stop** key.

Handy Hint

If your macro didn't work, you may have assigned it to Text for Task 1 and then closed the file without saving.

Run a macro assigned to a toolbar

You will now run the macro that was assigned to a toolbar. One method for doing this is:

Method

1 Click inside the first paragraph.

2 Select **Tools** from the main menu bar, then select: **Macro**: **Macros**. A Macros dialogue box appears, with a list of the macros you have recorded. You can delete any unwanted macros at this point.

3 Select the macro: **LDG_FIRST_PARA**.

4 Click on: **Run**. The formatting should be applied to the text.

One of the most common uses of macros is to record Page Setup details, particularly if the company you work for has a different layout for standard documents than the Word defaults, e.g. wide left-hand margins for hole punching, etc.

7.9 Assign a macro button to a toolbar or create a macro toolbar

You can also assign the macro to a button on the toolbar. You can assign a macro to any toolbar, but where you put it, to remember easily the formatting toolbar is possibly the best option.

Add a macro button to an existing toolbar

Method

1 Right-click on the Formatting Toolbar, select: **Customize**. The Customize dialogue box appears.

2 Click on the **Commands** tab.

3 In **Categories**, select: **Macros**.

4 In the **Commands** box, select the body text macro you want on the toolbar: **LDG_FIRST_PARA**.

Figure 7.20 Using the Customize dialogue box to assign a macro button to a toolbar

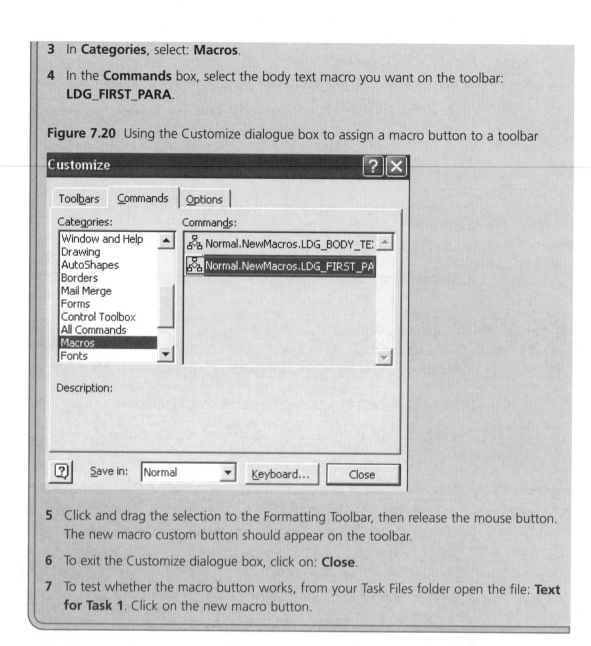

5 Click and drag the selection to the Formatting Toolbar, then release the mouse button. The new macro custom button should appear on the toolbar.

6 To exit the Customize dialogue box, click on: **Close**.

7 To test whether the macro button works, from your Task Files folder open the file: **Text for Task 1**. Click on the new macro button.

Be careful not to accidentally click on the macro button when you have a document on-screen that you don't want formatting. Undo does not work! If you have no use for the macro button, it is safer to remove it from the Formatting Toolbar. Click on the drop-down arrow at the end of the toolbar to add or remove buttons. If the macro is not available to remove, click on: **Reset Toolbar**.

Handy Hint

Always save your work just before you run a macro – you may not like the effect! If this is the case, you can revert to the saved version.

Create a macro toolbar

If you would rather have a macro toolbar than assign the macro to an existing toolbar, you can set one up.

Assign a macro button to a toolbar or create a macro toolbar

Method

1 Right-click on a toolbar to access the pop-up menu, then select: **Customize**.

2 In the **Customize** dialogue box, click on the **Toolbars** tab.

3 Click on: **New**. A **New Toolbar** dialogue box appears.

4 In the **Toolbar Name** box, type: **Macros**.

Figure 7.21 Create a new toolbar in the New Toolbar dialogue box

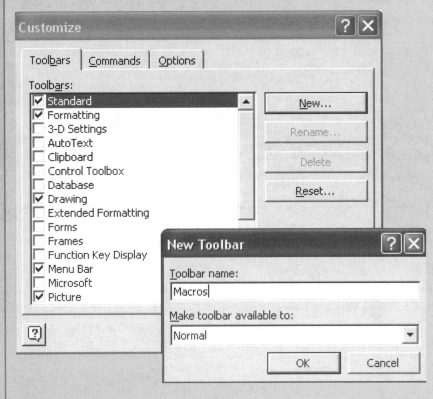

5 Click on: **OK**.

6 Click on: **Close**.

You should now have a small toolbar on your screen that you can assign buttons to as you did when you assigned the macro button to the Formatting Toolbar. If you click on: **View**: **Toolbars**, you will see listed the Macros Toolbar that you have just created.

7 Assign the two macros you have created to your new Macro Toolbar. Use the same method as above, but this time right-click on the Macro Toolbar. As before, click and drag the two macros (the two actions) to the Macro Toolbar.

8 Close the new toolbar by clicking on: **X**.

7.10 Copy a macro

There are occasions when you might want to copy a macro from one document to another without it being accessible through the toolbar or keyboard shortcut. To keep the macro within a document, you need to specify where the macro is to be stored when you are setting it up. In other words, you change the saving default from Normal.dot to the name of the document in which the macro is to be stored.

You are going to copy a macro named 'Header' which is stored in the file 'Macro Document' to the file 'Text for Task 1'. This macro is a line of text in a header 'Produced for the Literary Discussion Group'. However, the macro could easily be a standard paragraph, a disclaimer, or other sensitive text that you don't want to have instant access to for all documents.

Method

1 From the Task Files folder, open the file: **Text for Task 1**.

2 Select **Tools** from the main menu bar, then select: **Macro**: **Macros**.

3 In the **Macros** dialogue box, click on the **Organizer** button.

4 Select the **Macro Project Items** tab.

Figure 7.22 The Macro Project Items tab in Organizer

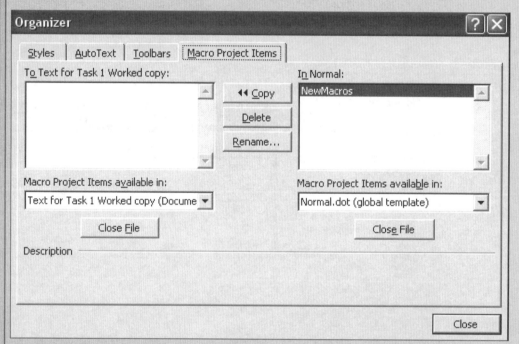

5 Click on both the **Close File** buttons so that you can make your own selections. The buttons change to **Open File**.

6 Click on the right-hand **Open File** button. This is the file that you are going to copy the macro from.

7 From the Task Files folder, select the file: **Macro Document**. To do this you may have to use the **Files of type** drop-down menu to change the selection to: **All Files**.

8 Click on the left-hand **Open File** button, then select the document: **Text for Task 1**.

9 On the **Copy** button, there should be two arrows pointing left. Click on this button and **NewMacros** is copied across to the other document.

Figure 7.23 Copying a macro from one document to a second document

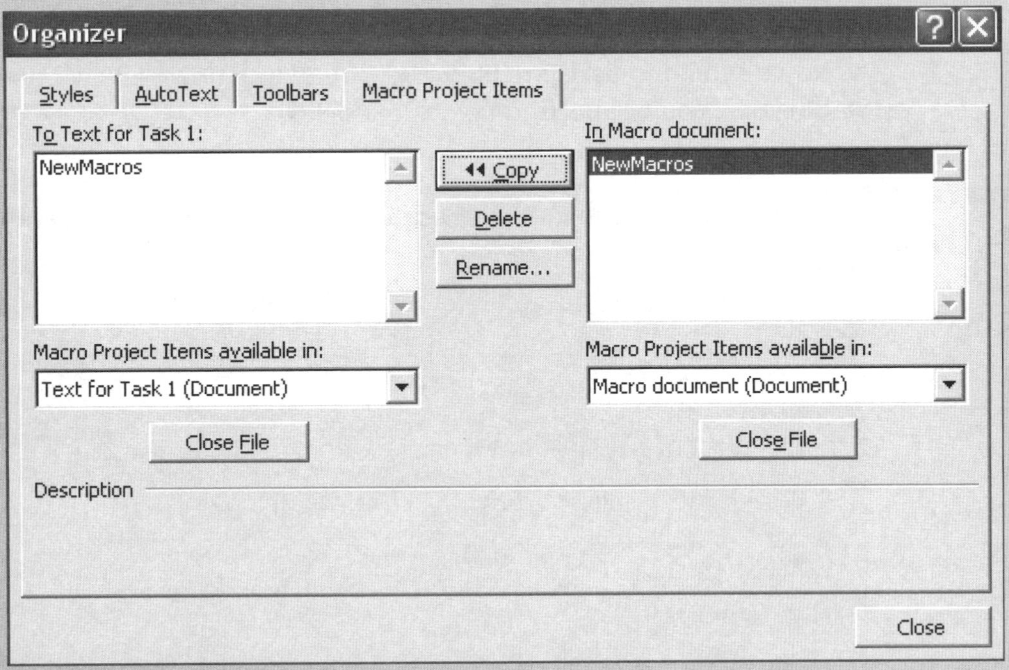

Note: the macro will not copy if the text 'NewMacros' already appears in the left-hand box. If it does, select the text and then click on the **Delete** button to remove the text. Next, click on the right-hand 'NewMacros' to make it active for copying to the other document. When prompted to delete, click on: **Yes**.

10 Click on: **Close**.

The macro is now within both documents but is not accessible for any other documents, for example, through Tools or Macro, etc.

You still need to go through the procedure of running the macro from the document Text for Task 1.

Method

1 Open the document: **Text for Task 1**.

2 Select **Tools** from the main menu bar, then select: **Macro**: **Macros**.

3 In the **Macros** dialogue box, click to select the macro named 'Header', then click on: **Run**. The Header should appear on-screen.

4 Save your work as: **Text for Task 1**.

Note: if you found that you could not run the macro due to the macros being disabled you will need to change the security setting. To do this click on: **Tools**: **Macro**: **Security** and change the level to medium. It is unlikely that you will be able to change security settings if you are working on a networked PC.

7.11 Amend or update field code entries

Some changes need to be made to the staff rota.

Remove Form Field options

Open the file: **Staff Rota**. Before you can make any changes, you will need to make sure that the fields are unlocked. If the drop-down arrow appears next to the staff names, you will need to unlock the fields.

Method

1 On the main menu toolbar, select: **View**, then select: **Toolbars**: **Forms**. The Form Toolbar appears on-screen.

2 Click on the **Protect Form** icon (i.e. unlock). The drop-down boxes disappear.

3 Double-click in the first shaded box: **Week 1**, **Monday**. The **Drop-Down Form Field Options** dialogue box appears.

P Wong is not available in Week 1: the name needs deleting.

4 Click on the name: **P Wong**, then click on: **Remove**.

Figure 7.24 Remove Form Field options using the Drop-Down Form Field Options dialogue box

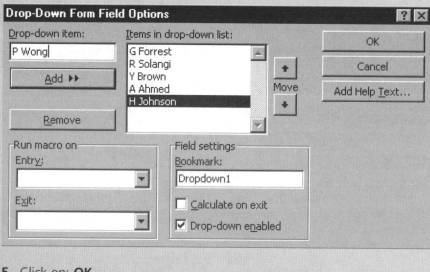

5 Click on: **OK**.

6 Repeat this method for Tuesday to Friday in Week 1.

Update date and time manually

The date and time are set to update automatically, i.e. when you open the file. You can update them manually.

Method

1 Select the **Date and Time** field.

2 Right-click to access the pop-up menu.

3 Select: **Update Field**.

Amend or update field code entries

Use AutoText

It would be useful to include a field with the filename so that you don't have to remember where you saved it. You can insert a field as you did for the date and time, but there is another way using AutoText.

Method

To include the filename and path and the date the document was created on:

1   Click at a point underneath the table.

2   From the main menu toolbar, select: **Insert**: **AutoText**: **Filename and path**.

Figure 7.25 Inserting an automatic text entry option

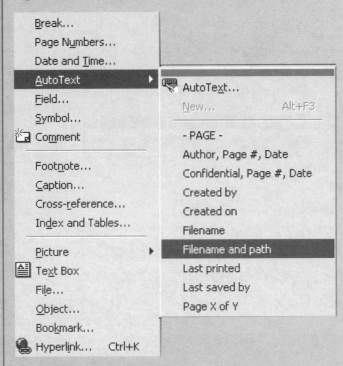

3   If you have already saved your work the name of the file will appear on your document at the insertion point. If you have not saved your work at this point, Word will insert the default filename: **Document?**.

To include an AutoText entry in the header that will show the date the document was created on, you need to select the header first.

Method

1   Click on: **View**: **Header and Footer**.

2   The I-beam cursor appears in the Header. In the **Header and Footer** dialogue box, click on: **Insert AutoText** to access the pop-up menu.

3   Select: **Created on**. The AutoText entry appears in the Header.

4   Click on: **Close**.

7.13　Use check boxes

You also need to include a check box for each member of staff on the rota that you can use to indicate when you have contacted them.

Method

1　Key in the names in a list underneath the table, e.g.

G Forrest
P Wong
R Solangi
Y Brown
A Ahmed
H Johnson

2　Click after each name and insert 2 spaces (to leave a space after the name).

3　On the Forms Toolbar, click on the **Check Box Form Field** icon.

Figure 7.26 The Check Box Form Field icon on the Forms Toolbar

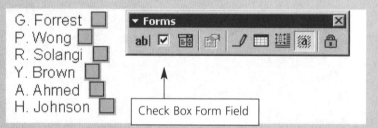

4　At the end of the name field, you should get a shaded square box.

5　Repeat this operation for the rest of the staff.

6　As with the drop-down fields, the check boxes don't work until the form is locked. Lock the form and see the effect that clicking in the boxes has. You should get a black cross when you click on the check boxes.

7.14　Delete items in a form (AM3.4.2.3)

It has been decided that no one is going to work on Friday in Week 4. This field needs deleting.

Method

1　Make sure that the form is not locked.

2　In the table, select the very last cell's drop-down field using the pointer tool.

3　Delete using the **Delete** key or right-click and select: **Cut**.

Figure 7.27 Select to delete a drop-down field in a form

ek 3	Week 4
orrest	G Forrest
orrest	G Forrest
orrest	G Forrest
orrest	G Forrest
orrest	G Forrest
57	

Note: double-clicking will not select the cell: it brings up the Options box. You need to position the pointer towards the bottom left-hand corner of the shaded area in the cell. When a black arrow appears, click to select.

If you are unsure if you have selected the field, to display the field code press: **Alt + F9**. Then press **Alt + F9** again to restore the text/numbers. The Alt + F9 shortcut is very useful if your fields are not shaded, i.e. if the Form Field Shading icon is not selected.

Try this now.

Method

1 Click on the **Form Field Shading** icon. The shading disappears from the document and it is difficult to see if you have any fields.

2 Press the keys: **Alt + F9**. The fields are displayed as code.

3 Press the keys: **Alt + F9** again to remove the code.

4 Click on the **Form Field Shading** icon to turn the field shading back on.

5 Lock your form, then: **Save**.

Practice Task

Task 7

These exercises are included to help the candidate in his or her training for the Advanced ECDL program. The exercises included in this material are not Advanced ECDL certification tests and should not be construed in any way as Advanced ECDL certification tests. For information about Authorised ECDL Test Centres in different National Territories, please refer to the ECDL Foundation website at **www.ecdl.com**.

Method

You are going to send a memo to all the people in the office that contributed to a local charity.

1 Amend the contemporary memo template by: (AM3.1.3.2)

   o Removing the grey shading (some of which is in the footer). (AM3.1.3.1)
   o Changing 'Memorandum' to 'Memo'.
   o Removing the 'cc' line.
   o Removing the 'click and type here' fields.

2 Save your new template in the Templates folder as: **Office memo**.

Save as Document template.

3 Close the document.

4 Set up the following table of contributions on a new page.

First name	Surname	Contribution
Julie	Smith	£2.00
James	Guest	£6.50
Richard	Stephens	£0.00
Susan	Bridge	£2.50
Gregory	Cobham	£4.00
Katherine	Duxbury	£0.00
John	Moss	£3.50
Ahmed	Akhtar	£4.50
Bernice	O'Sullivan	£5.20

5 Save your work as: **Charity data**.

6 Open up the Office Memo template and use Mail Merge Helper to merge the memo with the data. (AM3.5.1.3)

The Office Memo template is accessible from File: New: General.

The details you need for the memo are set out below:

To: <<First_Name>> <<Surname>>
From: Your name here
Date: Today's date
Re: Local charity

Thank you very much <<First_Name>> for the contribution of <<Contribution>>. It was greatly appreciated.

7 Sort the data in order of surname (AM3.5.1.2)

8 Filter out those people that did not contribute.

If you forget where you are up to with the Mail Merge, click on the Mail Merge Helper icon to bring the dialogue box on-screen.

Note: you can only do this up to the point before you click on the Merge buttons.

You should have seven merged memos; the first one should be to Ahmed Akhtar. If your Mail Merge has not worked, you should still have the data and the Form Letter saved, so that you can try again. You cannot 'Undo' merged documents.

9 Save your Mail Merge file as: **Task 7a Answer**.

10 Open a new document and record a simple macro to set up the following formatting:

- a landscape page
- 3 cm margins all around
- 3 columns with a line between
- the AutoText: **Confidential** in the top left-hand corner. (AM3.1.1.4)

Assign the macro to the toolbar. Name the macro: **A4 Land**. (AM3.5.2.1)

11 Assign the macro to a Custom button on the Formatting Toolbar. (AM3.5.2.4)

12 Close without saving.

13 Open the document: **Task 2 Answer**. Unlock it and save as: **Task 7b Answer**. Leave the file open.

14 Open a new blank document. Save the document as: **Disclaimer Text**.

15 Record another macro; name it: **Disclaimer**. Store the macro in: Disclaimer text (document). Record (key in) the following text using Times New Roman 12 pt font.

The restaurant reserves the right to amend or delete any of the set menus at anytime.

16 Go to the document Task 7b Answer. Copy the Disclaimer macro to it. (AM3.5.2.2)

17 Run the Disclaimer macro in the footer of Task 7b Answer. (AM3.5.2.3)

18 Update the File Name field in the last row of the table. (AM3.3.2.2)

19 Remove Set Menu 6 and Set Menu 7 from lunchtime. (AM3.4.2.1)

20 Split the cells in column 1. (AM3.4.1.1)

Handy Hint

Highlight rows 2–12. Remove the tick in: Merge cells before split.

21 So that you can indicate which week is the current week, insert a Check Box form field in the new column. (AM3.4.2.2)

22 Reduce the width of the column so that it just accommodates the check box.

23 In Weeks 1, 4 and 8 there is no lunchtime sitting: remove these fields. (AM3.4.2.3)

Task 8   *Personnel interviews*

In this task, you will cover the following skills:

- Track changes in a document.
  - o Change the formatting of tracked changes.
- Accept or reject changes.
- Add or remove comments.
- Edit comments.

Scenario

A new job has come in from personnel for checking. It is a quick simple job. They would like you to check the accuracy of the word processing skills of three interviewees. You already have the master document prepared and the candidates have saved their work to file.

8.1   *Track changes in a document*

You will track the changes in each of the candidates' files.

Method

1 From the Task Files folder, open the file with the first candidate's work: **Candidate 1**.

2 Click on: **Tools**: **Track Changes**, then select: **Compare Documents**. A dialogue box, Select File to Compare With Current Document, appears.

3 From the Task Files folder, select the file: **Personnel Master**.

Figure 8.1 Selecting a file to compare with current documents

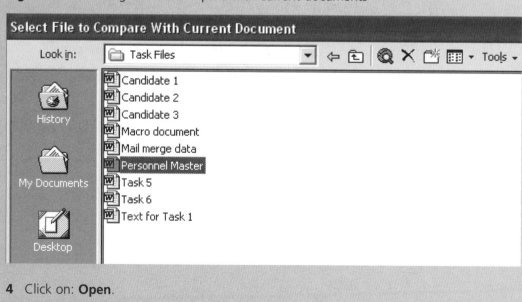

4 Click on: **Open**.

The file Personnel Master does not open but highlights (compares) the differences between the two documents by underscoring the errors on the candidate's document. Where an error occurs, Word inserts a straight vertical line marker in the right-hand margin.

Change the formatting of tracked changes

You can change the formatting of the tracked changes, for example, set them in a different colour.

Method

1 Click on: **Tools**: **Track Changes**, then select: **Highlight Changes**.

2 In the **Highlight Changes** dialogue box, select: **Options**. A Track Changes dialogue box appears.

3 Make your changes. As you make your selections, you can see the effect in the Preview boxes.

Figure 8.2 Change the formatting of tracked changes using the Track Changes dialogue box

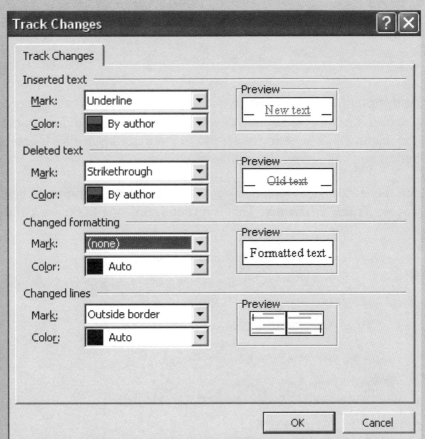

4 Click on: **OK** twice to exit the dialogue boxes. The changes should appear on your screen.

5 Repeat this method on the other two candidates' work.

6 Compare the documents and change the formatting of the changes. You will need to open candidate 2's work from the Task Files folder.

Accept or reject changes

The **Accept or Reject Changes** dialogue box is a useful tool if you are checking a long document and want to find the changes quickly. Try this on one of the candidate's work that you have already compared.

Method

With the candidate's work on screen:

1 Click on: **Tools**: **Track Changes**. The Accept or Reject Changes dialogue box appears.

2 Place the I-beam cursor at the top of the document. Click on the **Find button** with the right arrow to take you to the changes.

Figure 8.3 The Accept or Reject Changes dialogue box

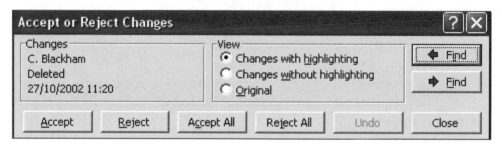

At this point you can decide whether to accept or reject the highlighted changes. If you click on the **Reject** button you will reject the candidate's amendments and the document will change to match the Personnel Master file. If you click on the **Accept** button you will accept the candidate's work.

Another feature of Track Changes is **Highlight Changes**, which is found under: **Tools: Track Changes**. This is a useful tool when you are editing existing work.

Method

1 Open the file: **Personnel Master**.

2 Click on: **Tools: Track Changes**, then select: **Highlight Changes**. A Highlight Changes dialogue box appears.

3 Click to select: **Track changes while editing**.

Figure 8.4 The Highlight Changes dialogue box

4 Click on: **OK**.

You will notice that the **Trk** button is now active on the status bar at the bottom on the screen.

5   Try adding text or deleting text from the document.

If you have the default options set, i.e. Inserted Text Mark is underline; Deleted Text-Mark is strikethrough, changes will appear in red and underscored as you key in. If these defaults are not set, your highlighting will look different.

6   Turn the tracking off by double-clicking on the **Trk** button.

7   Close this file without saving.

8.3   *Add or remove comments*

Now that you have viewed the candidates' work and seen the errors, you can add a comment to the file before you return the files to Personnel.

Method

1   Open the file: **Candidate 1**.

2   At the bottom of the document, you will see the words 'Candidate 1'. Highlight these words.

3   From the main menu toolbar, select: **View**: **Toolbars**: **Reviewing**. You should get a new toolbar underneath the Formatting Toolbar.

Figure 8.5 The Reviewing Toolbar

Insert Comment

4   Click on the yellow **Insert Comment** icon. A box is opened at the bottom of the screen for you to key in your comments on Candidate 1.

5   Key in: 'This candidate did not complete the work on time and had approximately 9 errors'.

Figure 8.6 Adding a comment to a document using the Insert Comment icon

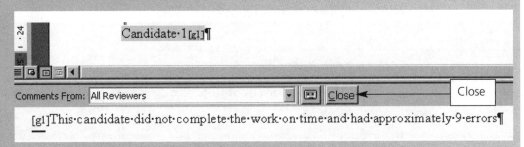

6   You will notice that just above the text box for your comments is the drop-down menu: **Comments From**. If you are working from your own PC, this drop-down menu would probably contain your name.

7   Click on: **Close**.

If you move the I-beam cursor over the highlighted Candidate 1 text, you will see the comment that you entered.

Figure 8.7 Move the cursor over the highlighted text to see the comment

> **gb20723:**
> This candidate did not complete the work on time and had approximately 9 errors
>
> Candidate·1 [g1]¶

8 Repeat this method with the other two candidates' work, putting in your comments. Suitable comments might be:

- **Candidate 2**: Work completed on time – 7 errors.
- **Candidate 3**: This candidate completed the least work and had 8 errors.

The **Cassette icon** to the right of **Comments From** is to add sound to the document. You could, if you had a microphone, record your comments as speech.

8.4 Edit comments

To edit text comments, there are two icons available to you on the Reviewing Toolbar:

- Edit Comment
- Delete Comment.

If you have no comments on your document, these two icons will not be available, i.e. they are shaded out.

Figure 8.8 The Edit Comment and Delete Comment icons on the Reviewing Toolbar

Edit Comment   Delete Comment

To edit or delete the text comment:

Method

1 Open the file: **Candidate 1**.

2 Click on the **Edit Comment** icon. This brings up the dialogue box with your comment in.

3 Click into this area and delete the words 'on time'.

4 Click on: **Close**.

Note: the Delete Comment option deletes the comment but leaves the original text, i.e. Candidate 1.

5 Click on the words 'Candidate 1'. This contains the text comment.

6 Click on the **Delete Comment** icon.

The comment is removed and both the Edit Comment and Delete Comment icons are now not available for use.

Practice Task

Task 8

These exercises are included to help the candidate in his or her training for the Advanced ECDL program. The exercises included in this material are not Advanced ECDL certification tests and should not be construed in any way as Advanced ECDL certification tests. For information about Authorised ECDL Test Centres in different National Territories, please refer to the ECDL Foundation website at **www.ecdl.com**.

Below is the draft text that is going to form the basis of a document to be sent out to help applicants complete the standard CV form.

1 In the Task Files Folder, open the file stored as: **Guidance notes**.

Guidance notes

It is essential to tell the truth on a CV as inaccurate or untrue information could lead at the very least to embarrassment or possibly to even more serious consequences. You are not obliged, however, to reveal every small detail of your private and not so private life. For example, if your GCSE grades were low, and you have not been asked to cite grades, simply present the subjects without the grades. It is important to be consistent here – you must not present some grades and not others. In actual fact, few employers will be really concerned about grades you received for exams taken many years ago. Although they will want to know that you have obtained certain qualifications, employers will be far more interested in your recent achievements.

If you are returning to work after a break, it is especially important for you to show that you have been doing interesting and relevant activities during your break from employment. This is because employers see less value in unpaid work than 9–5 paid employment. In your CV, you will need to talk about achievement, paid or unpaid, which you are proud off. Try to avoid emphasising duties that you have had to do and try to show how these activities would benefit the employer.

2 Add the following comment to the heading Guidance Notes: (AM3.1.4.1)

This is the first draft and must be revised by Personnel before distribution.

3 Make the following changes and use highlighting options to track the changes while editing. Make sure that the highlighting options you choose will show the changes when you print in black and white. (AM3.1.4.3)

- Expand CV to: Curriculum Vitae at the first occurrence.
- Delete the second sentence in the first paragraph.
- Add the following text as a new paragraph to the end of the document:

> REMEMBER: If you are not obliged to mention your weaker aspects, then avoid doing so.

- Change 'few employers will be' in the first paragraph to: 'we are not'.
- Change 'they' in the final sentence in the first paragraph to: 'we'.
- Change 'employers' in the final sentence in the first paragraph to: 'we'.
- Change the final word in the second paragraph, 'the employer', to: 'our company'.

4 Turn off the tracking.

5 Change the text comment to read: (AM3.1.4.2)

> This is the first draft and must be revised and approved by Personnel before distribution.

6 Save your work as: **Task 8 Answer**.

7 Print your work.

You should be able to see all the changes that you have made to the document.

In this task, you will cover the following skills:

- Create a Master Document.
- Use outline view.
- Add or delete subdocuments within a Master Document.
  - o Add files to a Master Document.
  - o Lock a Master Document.
  - o Display options.
  - o Delete a subdocument from a Master Document.
  - o Amend a subdocument in a Master Document.
  - o Change the order of subdocuments in a Master Document.
- Change existing character or paragraph styles.

- o Modify using the Style dialogue box.
- o Modify using the Outlining Toolbar.
- Create a subdocument from heading styles in a Master Document.
- Insert automatic captions.
  - o Select caption options.
  - o Insert ClipArt.
- Delete column breaks and section breaks.
- Add or delete a bookmark.
  - o Add a bookmark.
  - o Delete a bookmark.
- Add or delete a cross-reference.

Scenario

You have been given a job that is causing problems. Four people are contributing to the final document and thus it is becoming large and unmanageable. To make matters worse, not everyone has finalised their work and some people need to keep updating their sections.

9.1 | *Create a Master Document*

Master Documents are particularly useful when you are handling a large amount of text, e.g. a book. You can create each chapter or section as separate files and then, when the chapters are complete, bring them all together (as subdocuments) within the book (the Master Document). Working with smaller files (subdocuments) is very efficient: it reduces the time the PC needs to save the file down and makes it much easier to move from one chapter to the next.

Alternatively, you could bring together several files from several different people into one master document, e.g. a report. The subdocuments will link back to the contributor's original file(s).

The mechanics of creating a new Master Document are the final stages of 'work in progress'. In the scenario for this task you can create a Master Document that brings together all the sections as subdocuments but which also enables the four contributors to amend their own individual sections. The Master Document updates automatically each time it is opened.

Caution! Master Documents are not to be confused with templates or documents that you may refer to as a 'master'.

Note: before you start on this task you need to have the files you are going to be working with saved either on your PC (standalone PC) or in your home area (networked PC). The files you need to copy from the CD are in the **Task Files Directory**: **Ancient Egyptian Women**, **Egypt General**, **Egypt Social** and **Egypt Legal**. If you do not do this you will have problems saving the Master Document.

9.2 Use outline view

You have been given a separate file from each of the four contributors. Together, these will produce one large document on the subject of 'Woman in Ancient Egypt'. To do this, you will be working in Outline View.

Method

1 Open a new blank document.

2 Change the view of the document by clicking on: **View**: **Outline**. The **Outlining Toolbar** appears below the Formatting Toolbar.

Figure 9.1 The Outlining Toolbar

This is the basis of your Master Document.

9.3 Add or delete subdocuments within a Master Document

Adding files to a Master Document

The four separate Word files are now going to be combined to create a new Master Document. (AM3.2.1.1).

Method

1 Click on the **Insert Subdocument** icon.

2 In the **Insert Subdocument** dialogue box, select the file: **Ancient Egyptian Women**.

3 Click on: **Open**. The subdocument appears in the Master Document.

4 Scroll to the end of this subdocument.

5 Click underneath the text (outside the box) and you should have a flashing I-beam cursor.

6 Repeat the above sequence to add the files **Egypt General**, **Egypt Social** and **Egypt Legal** to the Master Document.

Note: when inserted, the subdocuments will pick up the formatting in the Master Document. This formatting will be changed later in the task.

In Outline View, documents looks very different. The main differences are that images do not appear and there are symbols to the left of the text.

1 Click on: **View**: **Print Layout**: **Print Preview** from the formatting toolbar.

2 Click on the **Multiple Pages** icon (fourth from left). Hold down the Shift key and, using the arrow keys, select: 2 × 4 pages. Press: **Enter**. You will see that all four documents are now together in one Master Document.

3 Click on: **Close** to go back to Print Layout View. If you have blank pages in your Master Document and you want to remove them, you can delete the section breaks at this stage by clicking on the **Show/Hide** icon, clicking on the **Section Break/Page Break** markers and pressing the **Delete** key.

4 Change back to Outline View.

Figure 9.2 Using Print Preview to view a Master Document

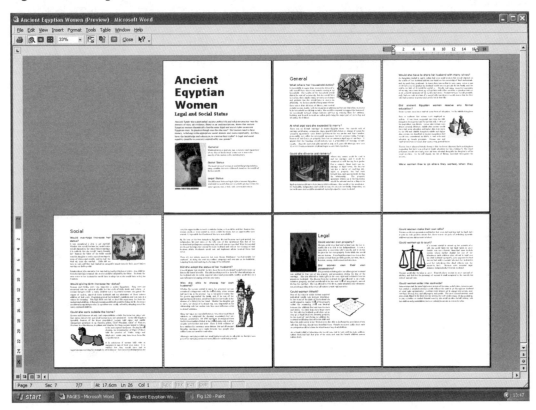

Lock a Master Document

You can lock the Master Document so that no amendments can be made to it.

Method

1 On the Outlining Toolbar, click on the **Lock Document** icon.

2 Save your new Master Document as: **Ancient Egyptian Women Master**.

Caution: you cannot lock the subdocuments within the Master Document if they are already open, for example, if a contributor is making amendments to the file or a subdocument is open on your PC. Word will lock only those subdocuments that are closed and will warn you that not all the subdocuments have been locked.

You should be able to see two small icons at the top left-hand side of each subdocument. The square one indicates the start of the subdocument; the 'lock' underneath shows that the subdocument is locked.

Figure 9.3 Icons to indicate that a subdocument is locked

Display options

One of the distinguishing features of Master Documents is that you can display your document as a list of file names.

Method

1 Click on the **Collapse Subdocuments** icon 🔁 .

Your document should have changed to show the subdocuments listed as links to where the document is stored.

Figure 9.4 Click on the Collapse Subdocuments icon to display the Master Document subdocument links

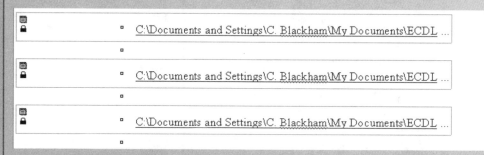

Caution: if this does not work, check that you are working on the file Ancient Egypt Women Master that you have saved to your PC.

Remember, documents inserted as subdocuments have not been moved or amended in any way; they have only been linked together to form the Master Document.

2 Check that the links work by double-clicking on one of the square subdocument icons. The page should now appear in Print Layout view.

3 From the main menu toolbar, select: **Window**. From the drop-down menu, to go back to the Master Document select: **Ancient Egyptian Women Master**.

4 With the four collapsed subdocuments on screen, click on: **Print Preview**. You will be asked if you want to expand the documents. Click on: **Yes**. The content of the Master Document appears in Print Preview.

5 Click on: **Close**.

6 The Master Document is now displayed in full in Outline View. To view the Master Document again as links, click on the **Collapse Subdocuments** icon.

You can expand the subdocuments using the same icon that you used to collapse them. Try this now. The name of the icon changes to **Expand Subdocuments**. Click on this icon to view all the subdocuments.

Delete a subdocument from a Master Document

You are going to delete the last subdocument.

In Outline View, with the subdocuments either collapsed or expanded:

1 Click on the square subdocument icon on the left-hand side of the screen alongside the last subdocument. This selects the link (the whole subdocument).

2 To remove, press the **Delete** key.

If you delete the wrong file you can undo, but you will need to unlock the Master Document first.

This method does not delete the original file, only the subdocument within the Master Document.

Amend a subdocument in a Master Document

You cannot make changes to a Master Document if the original file is open, e.g. if a contributor is making an amendment. When the contributor has saved and closed the file, the Master Document updates automatically the next time it is opened.

1 Show the Master Document links by clicking on the **Collapse Subdocuments** icon.

2 Click on the link to go to the second subdocument.

3 Delete the first subheading: 'What were her …'.

4 Save and close the subdocument.

Note: if you have changed the folder that the subdocument is stored in, you will see the link has changed to show the new pathway to the file.

5 Expand the Master Document and you should see that the subheading is missing from the second subdocument.

6 Save your work.

Caution: if the contributor renames or moves the file from the original location, the subdocument will disappear from the Master Document. You would need to reinsert the subdocument.

Change the order of subdocuments in a Master Document

Before you can change the order of the subdocuments, the Master Document needs to be unlocked. Word will tell you if you forget. The **Unlock** icon is the last button on the Outlining toolbar.

Figure 9.5 Remember to unlock a Master Document before changing the order of the subdocuments

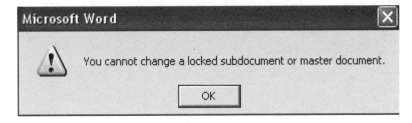

To unlock the Master Document, you must position the I-beam cursor outside the subdocument boxes.

Reordering the subdocuments is easier to do when the subdocuments are collapsed.

Method

1 On the document icon positioned in the top left-hand corner of the subdocument box, click and hold down the left mouse button.

2 Drag the icon to below the last subdocument.

Change existing character or paragraph styles

9.4

Modify using the Style dialogue box

A request has come to amend the body text on the subdocuments. To do this you are going to amend the existing style that is already applied to the text.

Method

1 Expand all the subdocuments.

2 Click in the first paragraph in the second subdocument.

3 Click into the body text underneath the subheading.

4 Click on: **Format**: **Style**. The Style dialogue box appears. You can see from this box that the name of the style you are going to amend is **Normal**.

Figure 9.6 The Style dialogue box

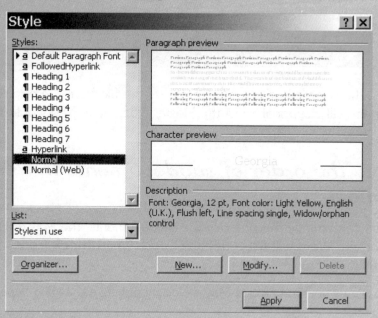

5 Click on: **Modify**. The Modify Style dialogue box appears.

6 Click on the **Format** drop-down menu. Select: **Font**.

Figure 9.7 Select Format: Font in the Modify Style dialogue box

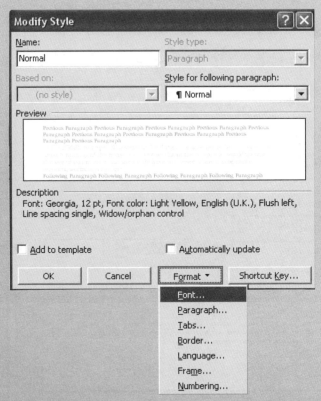

The **Font** dialogue box appears. Make the following amendments:

- Font: **Arial**
- Font style: **Regular**
- Size: **10 pt**
- Font color: **Dark Green** or a colour of your choice.

Figure 9.8 Selecting font options in the Font dialogue box

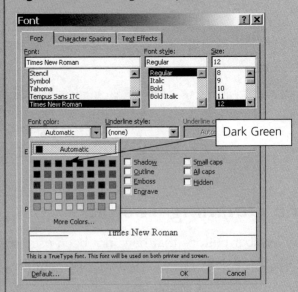

7 Click on: **OK** to return to the Modify Style dialogue box.

8 Click on: **Format**: **Paragraph**. The Paragraph dialogue box appears.

9 Make the following amendments:

- Special: **Hanging**
- Line spacing: **1.5 lines**.

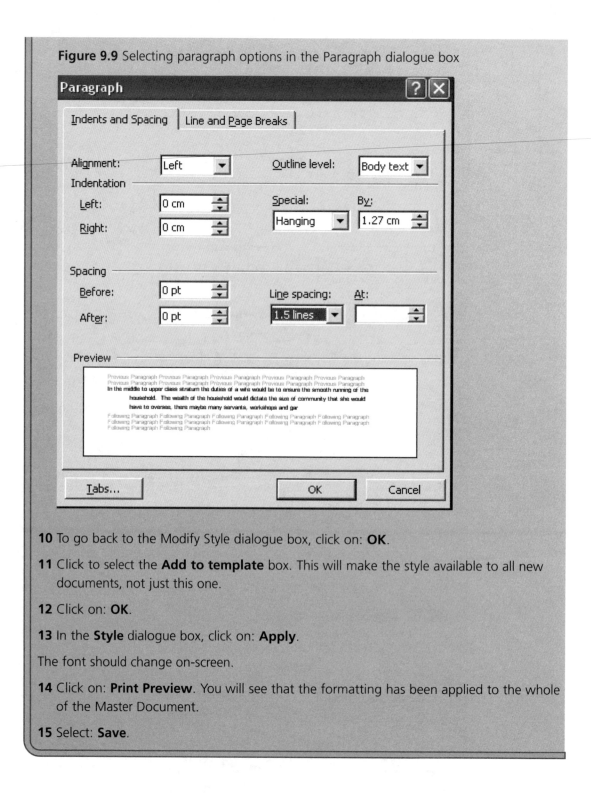

Figure 9.9 Selecting paragraph options in the Paragraph dialogue box

10 To go back to the Modify Style dialogue box, click on: **OK**.

11 Click to select the **Add to template** box. This will make the style available to all new documents, not just this one.

12 Click on: **OK**.

13 In the **Style** dialogue box, click on: **Apply**.

The font should change on-screen.

14 Click on: **Print Preview**. You will see that the formatting has been applied to the whole of the Master Document.

15 Select: **Save**.

Modify using the Outlining Toolbar

There are more Outlining Toolbar buttons that have not been used so far.

The first few buttons are: **Promote**; **Demote**; **Demote to Body Text**; **Move Up**; **Move Down**. These affect the position of the text.

Handy Hint

Unless you unlock the Master Document, not all the Outlining Toolbar buttons are available for use.

Change existing character or paragraph styles

Click into the text on the second subdocument. Click on the green arrows on the toolbar.

Figure 9.10 Modify text position icons on the Outlining Toolbar

Experiment by selecting the arrows in turn. To see the effect, click on: **Print Preview**. Undo your selections before you try the next one.

The next buttons (numbered 1–7) will display the headings that have been formatted using the Styles drop-down menu. If you click down on any of the headings you will see in the Style drop-down menu which heading style has been applied to that particular piece of text, e.g. Heading 1 (perhaps your subheading). If you then click on the numbered button 1, you will get a list of all the text that has the same style of formatting applied, i.e. you will get a list of all your subheadings. This is more evident when you set up a new Master Document with new subdocuments that you have applied styles to. The example you have been working on was a new Master Document using existing files as subdocuments.

The **All** button displays all the headings. The next icon displays the headings and the first line of text.

Close your work without saving.

9.5 Create a subdocument from heading styles in a Master Document

From the Task Files folder, open the file: **Poems**.

There are 10 poems in the document. Each of the poems needs to be in a separate file. This means that you are going to create 10 new subdocuments.

To create 10 subdocuments in one operation, the headings have to be formatted to a Word heading style.

Method

1 Save the Poems document to your PC. Name the file: **Poems2**.

2 Click in each of the poem titles in turn and, from the **Styles** drop-down menu, select: **Heading 1**.

Figure 9.11 From the Styles drop-down menu, select: Heading 1

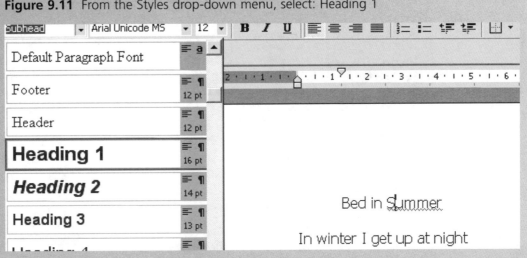

Your Heading 1 may not be the same format as the one in Figure 9.10. The important point is that each of the titles is formatted using the same style. If one of the titles is not formatted, then the poem will not become a subdocument.

Method

3 Click on: **View**: **Outline**.

4 Select all the poems – press: **Ctrl + A**.

5 Click on the **Create Subdocument** icon. If the icon is not available, check that you have saved your work to your PC.

The subdocuments should now be created. The poems have boxes around them.

Figure 9.12 Using the Create Subdocument icon to create subdocuments

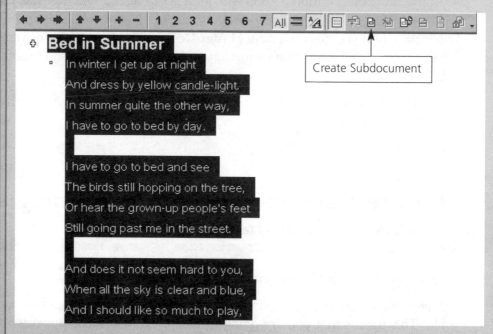

6 Click on the **Collapse Documents** icon (you may be asked to save) and you will see the links to the new subdocuments.

7 Click on one of the links and you will see that each poem is now a separate file.

8 If you click on: **File**: **Open** you should see the new subdocuments listed as separate files.

Figure 9.13 The new subdocuments listed as files in File: Open

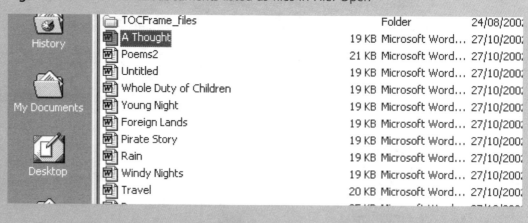

9 Save your work.

Create a subdocument from heading styles in a Master Document

Insert automatic captions

The document is not visually attractive and the pages would benefit from pictures being inserted.

Select caption options

Method

Click on: **View**: **Outline**. Make sure that the subdocuments are expanded and unlocked, and that you have the drawing toolbar at the bottom of your screen.

The AutoCaption needs to be made active so that you don't need to set the caption for each individual picture.

Method

1 Click on: **Insert**: **Caption**.

2 Click on: **Numbering**.

3 In the Caption Numbering dialogue box, from the Format drop-down menu, select: upper case Roman numerals.

Figure 9.14 The Caption and Caption Numbering dialogue boxes

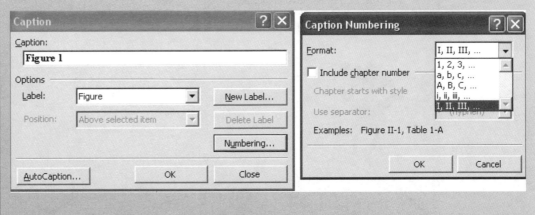

4 To close the Caption Numbering dialogue box, click on: **OK**.

5 Click on: **AutoCaption**.

6 Click on the box at the left-hand side to select: **Microsoft Word Picture**.

7 Click on: **OK**.

Insert ClipArt

The Microsoft Word Picture option was chosen because you are inserting ClipArt. If you were inserting slides from a presentation, the option to choose would be Microsoft PowerPoint Presentation.

8 Position the I-beam cursor at the end of the first poem (within the subdocument box).

9 On the Drawing Toolbar, click on the **Insert ClipArt** icon 🖻.

10 In the **ClipArt** dialogue box, click on: **Cartoons**. Select: **Clip 59** (next to the last option).

11 Click on: **Insert**.

12 Minimise the ClipArt Dialogue box.

The ClipArt should appear underneath the poem with the caption: Figure I.

13 Position the I-beam cursor underneath the second poem (in the second subdocument). Access the **ClipArt** dialogue box. From **Cartoons**, insert: **Clip 60**.

Figure 9.15 Insert ClipArt cartoons with selected caption numbering

Figure I

A Thought
It is very nice to think
The world is full of meat and drink,
With little children saying grace
In every Christian kind of place.

Figure II

14 Repeat this process for the remainder of the poems, inserting the following clips from cartoons:

- Subdocument 3: Clip 58 (beaches)
- Subdocument 4: Clip 54 (faces)
- Subdocument 5: Clip 10 (animals)
- Subdocument 6: Clip 38 (buildings)
- Subdocument 7: Clip 51 (oars)
- Subdocument 8: Clip 56 (persons)
- Subdocument 9: Clip 4 (canines)
- Subdocument 10: Clip 45 (air)

15 Click on: **Collapse Documents**.

16 Save your work.

17 Click on the subdocument links. There should be a captioned ClipArt picture on each page.

18 Close your Master Document and any subdocuments that are open.

9.7 Delete column breaks and section breaks

The Literary Discussion Group have brought back their Daniel Defoe document. They do not like the large gap on the first page and want it removing.

It is the same operation for both column and section breaks.

Method

1 Open your last saved copy of **Task 1**. It should look like Figure 9.15.

Figure 9.16 Open the file: Task 1

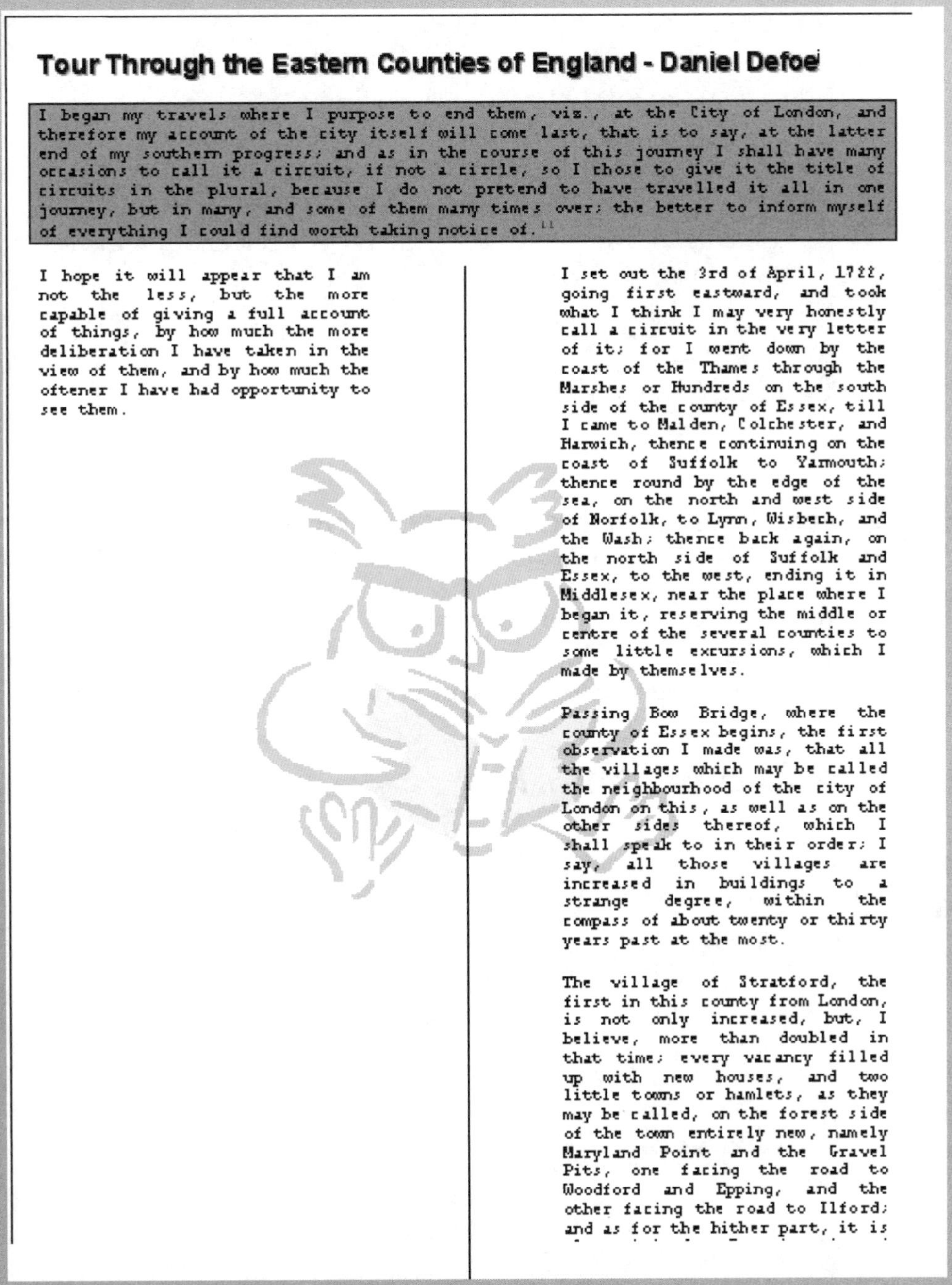

Tour Through the Eastern Counties of England - Daniel Defoe

I began my travels where I purpose to end them, viz., at the City of London, and therefore my account of the city itself will come last, that is to say, at the latter end of my southern progress; and as in the course of this journey I shall have many occasions to call it a circuit, if not a circle, so I chose to give it the title of circuits in the plural, because I do not pretend to have travelled it all in one journey, but in many, and some of them many times over; the better to inform myself of everything I could find worth taking notice of.

I hope it will appear that I am not the less, but the more capable of giving a full account of things, by how much the more deliberation I have taken in the view of them, and by how much the oftener I have had opportunity to see them.

I set out the 3rd of April, 1722, going first eastward, and took what I think I may very honestly call a circuit in the very letter of it; for I went down by the coast of the Thames through the Marshes or Hundreds on the south side of the county of Essex, till I came to Malden, Colchester, and Harwich, thence continuing on the coast of Suffolk to Yarmouth; thence round by the edge of the sea, on the north and west side of Norfolk, to Lynn, Wisbech, and the Wash; thence back again, on the north side of Suffolk and Essex, to the west, ending it in Middlesex, near the place where I began it, reserving the middle or centre of the several counties to some little excursions, which I made by themselves.

Passing Bow Bridge, where the county of Essex begins, the first observation I made was, that all the villages which may be called the neighbourhood of the city of London on this, as well as on the other sides thereof, which I shall speak to in their order; I say, all those villages are increased in buildings to a strange degree, within the compass of about twenty or thirty years past at the most.

The village of Stratford, the first in this county from London, is not only increased, but, I believe, more than doubled in that time; every vacancy filled up with new houses, and two little towns or hamlets, as they may be called, on the forest side of the town entirely new, namely Maryland Point and the Gravel Pits, one facing the road to Woodford and Epping, and the other facing the road to Ilford; and as for the hither part, it is

If you can't find it, there is a copy of the file on your CD in the Suggested Answers folder. It is named: **Task 1 with column break**.

2 Click on the **Show/Hide** icon to reveal the column and section breaks.

3 Select the column break underneath the text in column 1 by clicking in it.

Figure 9.17 Click on the Column Break to select

```
view·of·them,·and·by·how·much·the·          coast··of·
oftener·I·have·had·opportunity·to·          Marshes·o
see·them.··¶                                side·of·tl
                                            I·came·to
                                            Harwich,·t
·············Column Break·················  coast··of·
                                            thence··ro
                                            sea,··on·t
                                            of·Norfoll
                                            the·Wash·
```

4 Press the delete key.

The text should move from column 2 into column 1.

5 Remove the page break from page 3 using the same method as above.

Handy Hint

Take care that you only delete the page break and not the section break too. You will lose your column formatting if you do.

6 Save your work.

9.8 Add or delete a bookmark

You have been informed that more text is going to be added to Task 1 at a later date. The subject of the text will be Colchester. If you insert a bookmark in the text, you will be able to find the insertion point for the new text quickly.

Add a bookmark

Method

1 Click on: **Edit**: **Find**. The Find and Replace dialogue box appears.

Using the **Find** tab, search for the word: **Colchester**. You will see that there are many instances of the word. You are going to bookmark the instance where 'Colchester' is the first word of the paragraph (see Figure 9.17).

Figure 9.18 Bookmark where 'Colchester' is the first word of the paragraph

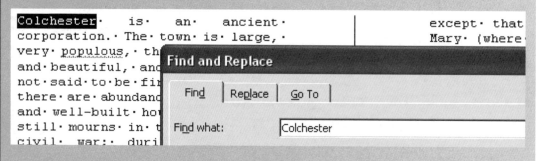

2 Exit Find and Replace by clicking on: **Cancel**.

3 Highlight to select the word Colchester.

4 Click on: **Insert**: **Bookmark**. A Bookmark dialogue box appears.

5 Key in the name of the bookmark, i.e. **Colchester_Insertion_Point**.

Figure 9.19 Key in the name of the bookmark in the Bookmark dialogue box

You cannot use spaces to separate the words, you must use the underscore key (as you did when you were naming macros).

6 Click on: **Add**.

The bookmark will be inserted. It is not obvious on the document even if you run the cursor over the insertion point.

To test if your bookmark is working:

Method

1 Click on: **Edit**: **Find**. The Find and Replace dialogue box appears.

2 Select the **Go To** tab.

3 In the **Go to what** box, select: **Bookmark**.

4 From the **Enter bookmark name** drop-down menu, select your bookmark: **Colchester_Insertion_Point**.

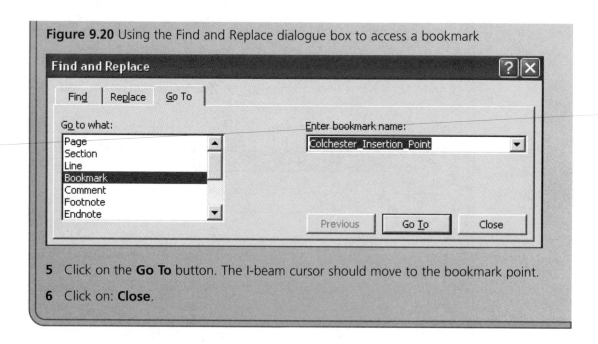

Figure 9.20 Using the Find and Replace dialogue box to access a bookmark

5 Click on the **Go To** button. The I-beam cursor should move to the bookmark point.

6 Click on: **Close**.

Delete a bookmark

Deleting the bookmark is exactly the same procedure as adding a bookmark:

Method

1 Click on: **Insert**: **Bookmark**. A Bookmark dialogue box appears.

2 In the **Bookmark** dialogue box, select the bookmark you want to delete.

3 Click on: **Delete**.

Figure 9.21 To delete a bookmark, select and click on the Delete button

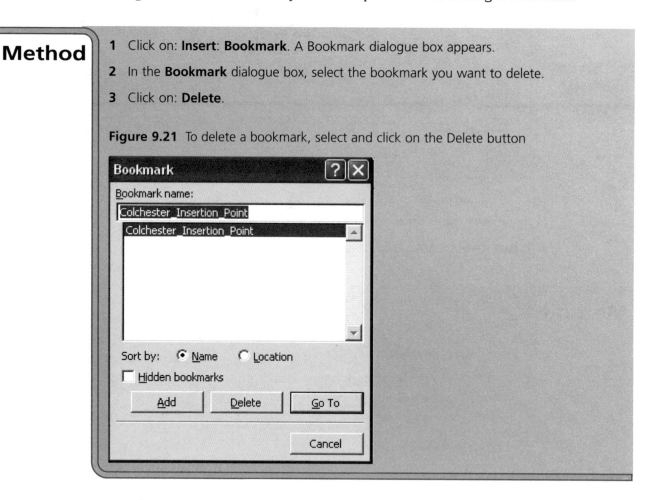

Do <u>not</u> delete the bookmark you have just created for Task 1.

Add or delete a cross-reference

Adding a cross-reference enables you to direct the reader to another piece of relevant information in the same document. You are going to cross-reference (link) a paragraph about the county Essex to the Colchester bookmark.

Method

1 Click at the end of paragraph 4 (that starts 'Passing Bow Bridge').

2 Press the **Enter** key twice to leave a clear line space.

3 In the space that you have just created, key in: **See notes on**:

4 Click on: **Insert**: **Cross-reference**. A Cross-reference dialogue box appears.

5 From the **Reference type** drop-down menu, select: **Bookmark**.

6 From the **Insert reference to** drop-down menu, select: **Bookmark text**.

7 Click to activate the **Insert as hyperlink** box.

8 Select the bookmark: **Colchester_Insertion_Point**.

9 Click on: **Insert**.

10 Click on: **Close**.

Handy Hint

If you underline the text **See notes on Colchester**, it will be more obvious that the text is a link. Be careful not to click on the word 'Colchester' as the link will take you straight to the Colchester_Insertion_Point bookmark.

If you want to delete the bookmark and practise again, select the underlined text 'See notes on Colchester' and press the delete key.

Save your work and close the file.

Task 9

These exercises are included to help the candidate in his or her training for the Advanced ECDL program. The exercises included in this material are not Advanced ECDL certification tests and should not be construed in any way as Advanced ECDL certification tests. For information about Authorised ECDL Test Centres in different National Territories, please refer to the ECDL Foundation website at **www.ecdl.com**.

You are going to create a Master Document that contains all your consolidation exercises in one file. (AM3.2.1.1)

1 Open a new document. Using Outline options, insert all your Practice Task Answer files as subdocuments. (AM3.1.2.6 & AM3.2.1.3)

2 When you insert Task 3 Answer, you may be asked if you want to 'Rename the style in the subdocument'; click on: No.

Some of the subdocuments look empty; this is because they contain images that are not visible in Outline view.

3 Lock the Master Document.

4 Save as: **Task 9a Master Document**.

5 Collapse the subdocuments and save your work.

6 Remove the first subdocument. (AM3.2.1.3)

7 Collapse the Master Document.

8 Open the collapsed subdocument 6 and amend the verse title subheading style to: (AM3.1.2.5)

   - Font: Britannic
   - Font style: Bold
   - Color: Violet

9 Amend the body text style to: (AM3.1.2.5)

   - Indentation: first line, 1 cm

10 Save your work and close the file.

11 Open the file: **Task 6 Answer**.

12 Create subdocuments from each of the fables. (AM3.2.1.2)

Handy Hint

Select only the fables, i.e. not the front page or the table of contents.

Note: if you get the message 'the selection does not consist of heading levels' you will need to apply a heading level to create the subdocuments. In Print Layout view, click down on one of the fable titles (style Verse Title). Click on: Format (main toolbar): Style: Modify: Format: Paragraph, then change the Outline level to Level 1. Click on: OK: OK: Apply. Change back to Outline view and try again.

13 Print the Outline view of the collapsed Master Document.

14 Using the Automatic Captions, insert a picture from ClipArt into at least four of the fables. (AM3.4.6.3)

Handy Hint

Insert the images in Outline view with the subdocuments expanded. Make sure that the original document is closed.

15 Save the file as: **Task 9b Answer**.

16 Print: 2 pages, 2 per sheet.

17 Close your file.

18 Open the file: **Task 3 Answer**.

19 Insert a picture from ClipArt. Search for clips relating to the moon, then select the ClipArt of the white moon on the black disk.

20 Position the ClipArt on page 2 in the gutter between columns 2 and 3.

21 Wrap the text so that it fits tightly around the disk. (AM3.1.1.6)

146   **Practice Task 9**

You will need to do this in Print Layout view.

22 Increase the size of the image to: Height 7 cm, Width 7 cm.

23 Print the current page.

24 Save as: **Task 9c Answer**. Close the file.

25 Open the file: **Task 6 Answer**.

26 Use Find to locate the word: Hercules.

27 Add a bookmark. (AM3.3.1.1)

28 Name the bookmark: Hercules Fable.

Don't forget to use underline to create the space between the words.

29 Test the bookmark to see if it works (Edit: Go To: Bookmark).

30 Using the Hercules Fable bookmark, cross-reference the fable 'The Lion and the Mouse' to the fable 'Hercules and the Wagon'. Insert a hyperlink after the fable title, i.e. after 'The Lion and the Mouse'. (AM3.3.1.3)

31 Index the following words:

- mouse
- boy
- child
- girl
- dog
- bear
- fox
- mole
- lion
- grasshopper
- bat.

There will not be entries for all letters until the remainder of the fables are input. (AM3.3.1.2)

32 Place the index at the end of the fables, before the table of contents. Mark all the entries.

33 Format page numbers to bold.

34 Apply the format: Classic.

35 Print the last 2 pages, 2 per page.

36 Save as: **Task 9d Answer**.

Answers to practice tasks

Task 1 Answer

MADRID

Panoramic Madrid

The history of the majestic city of Madrid will come to life when you allow your guide to introduce you to its incredible past. Once an Arabian Fortress, this city is now a thriving cultural centre bursting with monuments, galleries and museums. You will even see Santiago Bernabeu Stadium, home of the famous Real Madrid football team.

Artistic Madrid

Introducing one of the world's greatest art galleries. The Prado Museum holds major works from all the great schools of European art, including paintings by Rubens, Rafael, Goya, and El Greco. Let our guides take you there. Then move on to explore the 18th-century Royal Palace.

Toledo, El Escorial, Valley of the Fallen

Journey south of Madrid into a long forgotten world as you discover the ancient city of Toledo, once the medieval capital of Spain. Become familiar with the life of a monk as you tour El Escorial Monastery, and spare some thought for the dead of the Spanish Civil War in the Valley of the Fallen - the history of this country will simply amaze you.

Madrid by Night

At night, Spaniards put on their dancing shoes and step out for an evening of fun, feasting, and friendly flirting. After a panoramic drive to see the city lights, you'll join the locals at the Florida Park nightclub. Enjoy a fabulous tapas meal, a flamenco show, and all-night dancing.♥

♥ See Leaflet 6

Task 2 Answer

SET MENU PLANNER

19/01/2003		
	LUNCHTIME	EVENING
WEEK 1	Menu 1	Menu 1
WEEK 2	Menu 1	Menu 1
WEEK 3	Menu 1	Menu 2
WEEK 4	Menu 1	Menu 3
WEEK 5	Menu 1	Menu 4
WEEK 6	Menu 1	Menu 5
WEEK 7	Menu 1	Menu 6
WEEK 8	Menu 1	Menu 7
WEEK 9	Menu 1	Menu 8
WEEK 10	Menu 1	Menu 9
WEEK 11	Menu 1	Menu 10
WEEK 12	Menu 1	Menu 11
	Task 2 Answer	Menu 12

C. Blackham18/01/2003 16:57

Task 3 Answer

MADRID

Panoramic Madrid

The history of the majestic city of Madrid will come to life when you allow your guide to introduce you to its incredible past. Once an Arabian Fortress, this city is now a thriving cultural centre bursting with monuments, galleries and museums. You will even see Santiago Bernabeu Stadium, home of the famous Real Madrid football team.

Art in Madrid

Introducing one of the world's greatest art galleries. The Prado Museum holds major works from all the great schools of European art, including paintings by Rubens, Rafael, Goya, and El Greco. Let our guides take you there. Then move on to explore the 18th-century Royal Palace.

Toledo, El Escorial, Valley of the Fallen

Journey south of Madrid into a long forgotten world as you discover the ancient city of Toledo, once the medieval capital of Spain. Become familiar with the life of a monk as you tour El Escorial Monastery, and spare some thought for the dead of the Spanish Civil War in the Valley of the Fallen - the history of this country will simply amaze you.

¹ See Leaflet 3

Madrid by Night

At night, Spaniards put on their dancing shoes and step out for an evening of fun, feasting, and friendly flirting. After a panoramic drive to see the city lights, you'll join the locals at the Florida Park nightclub. Enjoy a fabulous tapas meal, a flamenco show, and all-night dancing. *

Task 4 Answer

Phantom of the Opera

PROLOGUE

The Opera ghost really existed. He was not, as was long believed, a creature of the imagination of the artists, the superstition of the managers, or a product of the absurd and impressionable brains of the young ladies of the ballet, their mothers, the box-keepers, the cloak-room attendants or the concierge. Yes, he existed in flesh and blood, although he assumed the complete appearance of a real phantom; that is to say, of a spectral shade.

When I began to ransack the archives of the National Academy of Music I was at once struck by the surprising coincidences between the phenomena ascribed to the "ghost" and the most extraordinary and fantastic tragedy that ever excited the Paris upper classes; and I soon conceived the idea that this tragedy might reasonably be explained by the phenomena in question. The events do not date more than thirty years back; and it would not be difficult to find at the present day, in the foyer of the ballet, old men of the highest respectability, men upon whose word one could absolutely rely, who would remember as though they happened yesterday the mysterious and dramatic conditions that attended the kidnapping of Christine Daae, the disappearance of the Vicomte de Chagny and the death of his elder brother, Count Philippe, whose body was found on the bank of the lake that exists in the lower cellars of the Opera on the Rue-Scribe side. But none of those witnesses had until that day thought that there was any reason for connecting the more or less legendary figure of the Opera ghost with that terrible story.

GASTON LEROUX

Task 5 Answer

Holidays in the Sun 1

7-night holidays

Dates	7 nights (£)	Extra night (£)	8 nights
10 May–23 May	210	21	£ 231.00
12 Apr–9 May	340	18	£ 358.00
30 Aug–5 Sep	337	26	£ 363.00
21 Jun–4 Jul	398	39	£ 437.00
24 May–6 Jun	420	28	£ 448.00
5 Jul–18 Jul	440	44	£ 484.00
7 Jun–20 Jun	460	34	£ 494.00
	£ 313.13		£ 340.38

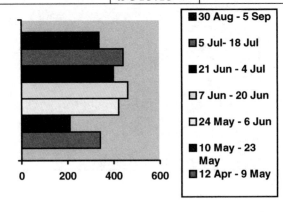

■ 30 Aug - 5 Sep

■ 5 Jul- 18 Jul

■ 21 Jun - 4 Jul

□ 7 Jun - 20 Jun

□ 24 May - 6 Jun

■ 10 May - 23 May

■ 12 Apr - 9 May

Task 6 Answer

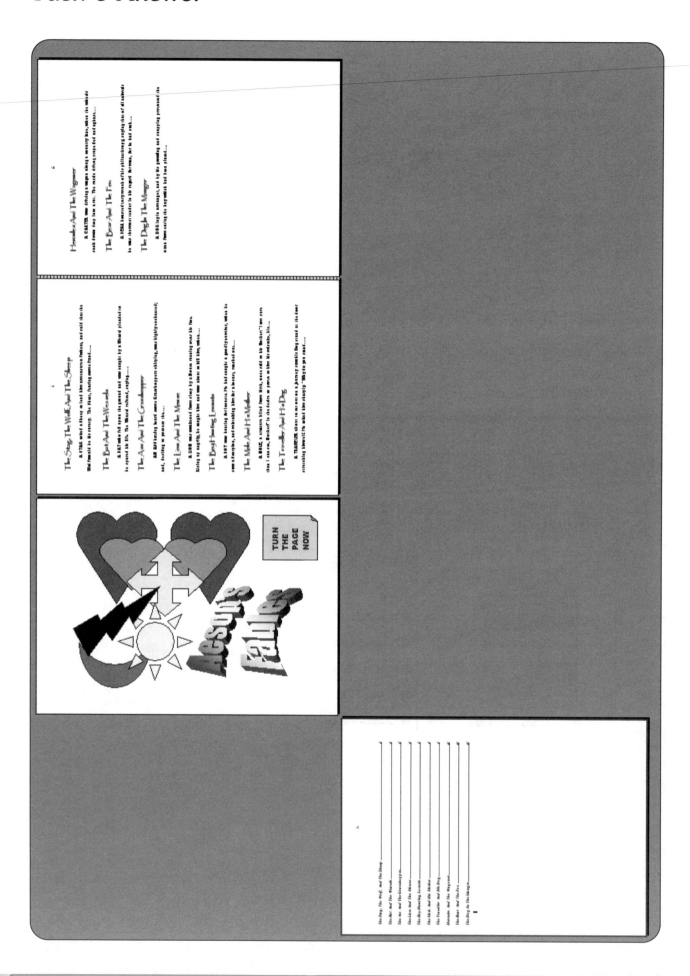

Answers to practice tasks

Task 7a Answer

FORM MEMO (LETTER)

Memo

To: «First_Name» «Surname»

From: Your name here

Date: Today's date

Re: Local Charity

_____

Thank you very much «First_Name» for the contribution of «Contribution». It was greatly appreciated.

MERGED MEMO

Memo

To: Julie Smith

From: Christine Blackham

Date:

Re: Local Charity

_____

Thank you very much Julie for the contribution of £2.00. It was greatly appreciated.

(You should have 7 memos)

Task 7b Answer

SET MENU PLANNER

		19/01/2003	
		LUNCHTIME	EVENING
WEEK 1	☐		Menu 1
WEEK 2	☐	Menu 1	Menu 1
WEEK 3	☐	Menu 1	Menu 1
WEEK 4	☐		Menu 1
WEEK 5	☐	Menu 1 ▾	Menu 1
WEEK 6	☐	Menu 1	Menu 1
WEEK 7	☐	Menu 2	Menu 1
WEEK 8	☐	Menu 3	Menu 1
WEEK 9	☐	Menu 4	Menu 1
WEEK 10	☐	Menu 5	Menu 1
WEEK 11	☐	Menu 8	Menu 1
WEEK 12	☐	Menu 9	Menu 1
		Menu 10	
		Menu 11	
		Menu 12	

Week 12 Lunchtime: Menu 1

Task 7 Answer

C. Blackham19/01/2003 16:04 The Restaurant reserves the right to amend or delete any of the set menus at anytime.

Task 8 Answer

GUIDANCE NOTES[g1]

It is essential to tell the truth on a Curriculum Vitae as inaccurate or untrue information could lead at the very least to embarrassment or possibly to even more serious consequences. ~~You are not obliged, however, to reveal every small detail of your private and not so private life.~~ For example, if your GCSE grades were low, and you have not been asked to cite grades, simply present the subjects without the grades. It is important to be consistent here - you must not present some grades and not others. In actual fact, ~~few employers will be~~we are not really concerned about grades you received for exams taken many years ago. Although ~~they~~we will want to know that you have obtained certain qualifications, ~~employers~~we will be far more interested in your recent achievements.

If you are returning to work after a break it is especially important for you to show that you have been doing interesting and relevant activities during your break from employment. This is because employers see less value in unpaid work than 9-5 paid employment. In your C.V. you will need to talk about achievement, paid or unpaid, which you are proud off. Try to avoid emphasising duties that you have had to do and try to show how these activities would benefit ~~the employer~~our company.

REMEMBER: If you are not obliged to mention your weaker aspects, then avoid doing so.

Task 9b Answer (Printout 1)

C:\Documents and Settings\C. Blackham\My Documents\The Stag.doc

C:\Documents and Settings\C. Blackham\My Documents\The Bat And The Weasels.doc

C:\Documents and Settings\C. Blackham\My Documents\The Ass And The Grasshopper.doc

C:\Documents and Settings\C. Blackham\My Documents\The Lion And The Mouse.doc

C:\Documents and Settings\C. Blackham\My Documents\The Boy Hunting Locusts.doc

C:\Documents and Settings\C. Blackham\My Documents\The Mole And His Mother.doc

C:\Documents and Settings\C. Blackham\My Documents\The Traveller And His Dog.doc

C:\Documents and Settings\C. Blackham\My Documents\Hercules And The Wagoner.doc

C:\Documents and Settings\C. Blackham\My Documents\The Bear And The Fox.doc

C:\Documents and Settings\C. Blackham\My Documents\The Dog In The Manger.doc

Task 9b Answer (Printout 2)

The Stag, The Wolf, And The Sheep

A STAG asked a Sheep to lend him a measure of wheat, and said that the Wolf would be his surety. The Sheep, fearing some fraud.....

Figure 1

The Bat And The Weasels

A BAT who fell upon the ground and was caught by a Weasel pleaded to be spared his life. The Weasel refused, saying.......

The Ass And The Grasshopper

AN ASS having heard some Grasshoppers chirping, was highly enchanted; and, desiring to possess the.....

Figure 2

The Lion And The Mouse

A LION was awakened from sleep by a Mouse running over his face. Rising up angrily, he caught him and was about to kill him, when.....

Figure 3

The Boy Hunting Locusts

A BOY was hunting for locusts. He had caught a goodly number, when he saw a Scorpion, and mistaking him for a locust, reached out.....

The Mole And His Mother

A MOLE, a creature blind from birth, once said to his Mother "I am sure that I can see, Mother!" In the desire to prove to him his mistake, his.....

The Traveller And His Dog

A TRAVELLER about to set out on a journey saw his Dog stand at the door stretching himself. He asked him sharply: "Why do you stand.....

Figure 4

Task 9c Answer

Toledo, El Escorial, Valley of the Fallen

Journey south of Madrid into a long forgotten world as you discover the ancient city of Toledo, once the medieval capital of Spain. Become familiar with the life of a monk as you tour El Escorial Monastery, and spare some thought for the dead of the Spanish Civil War in the Valley of the Fallen

---

♥ See Leaflet 3

- the history of this country will simply amaze you.

Madrid by Night

At night, Spaniards put on their dancing shoes and step out for an evening of fun, feasting, and friendly flirting. After a panoramic drive to see the city lights, you'll join the locals at the Florida Park nightclub. Enjoy a fabulous tapas meal, a flamenco show, and all-night dancing. ♥

Task 9d Answer

...... ii

The Bear And The Fox

A CARTER was driving a wagon along a country lane, when the wheels sank down deep into a rut. The rustic driver, stupefied and aghast....

A BEAR boasted very much of his philanthropy, saying that of all animals he was the most tender in his regard for man, for he had such....

The Dog In The Manger

A DOG lay in a manger, and by his growling and snapping prevented the oxen from eating the hay which had been placed....

B

Bat ii v
Bear, iii v
Boy, ii v

D

Dog ii iii v

F

Fox, iii v

G

Grasshopper, ii v

L

Lion ii v

M

Mole, ii v
Mouse, ii v

Practice assignment

These exercises are included to help the candidate in his or her training for the Advanced ECDL program. The exercises included in this material are not Advanced ECDL certification tests and should not be construed in any way as Advanced ECDL certification tests. For information about Authorised ECDL Test Centres in different National Territories, please refer to the ECDL Foundation website at **www.ecdl.com**.

There is a maximum of 20 marks for each question.

You are to:

- amend a document stored on your CD as: **Samuel Pepys**
- create a chart from data saved on your CD as **Table**
- perform a Mail Merge operation.

1 From the Task Files folder, open the document: **Samuel Pepys**.

2 To the heading 'Samuel Pepys', apply a $4\frac{1}{2}$ point box border.

3 Find the word 'shorthand' in the final paragraph, and position it at the start of the next line. At this point, from the Task Files folder, insert the image: 'shorthand'. Position the image to the right.

4 Below the image, add the caption: Pepys' shorthand.

5 Modify the existing style, Pepys Body Text, to Arial 12 pt. Apply the appropriate formatting so that single lines of text are not left at the top or bottom of the pages.

6 Apply a 2-column format to the paragraphs 'March 1st' and 'March 6th'.

7 Underneath the subheading Contents, create a table of contents based on the style Samuel Pepys Subheading, ensuring that all the diary dates are included. Apply the Fancy format and right-align the page numbers.

8 Apply the Samuel Pepys Subheading style to diary dates February 23rd and May 16th. Update your table of contents.

9 Record a macro to set up the page as landscape with 4 cm inside and outside and 2 cm top and bottom margins. Name the macro: Samuel Pepys. Apply the macro to this document only. Run the Macro.

10 Correct the Old English (Word has underlined the spelling errors) by keying in the more modern spelling to the right of the word. Track the changes while editing. Ensure that the editing can be seen on-screen and will be visible when printed. Turn off the Track Changes tool.

11 To the last word in the last paragraph, add the text comment: This was the last diary entry.

12 On the first line of April 26th, bookmark the word 'Fire'. Name the bookmark: Fire.

13 Underneath the words 'Completed the Exercise?' at the end of the document, insert a Yes/No drop-down selection box.

14 Above the word 'Contents', insert the year '1669' in a text box. Use Arial, 48 pt. Change the direction of the text so that the text runs from bottom to top. Ensure that there is not a box around the text.

15 Include an index as the final page of the document. Apply the Modern format. Mark the following words: God, Lord, wife, Deb, Duke, King, tailor.

16 Apply a WordArt style to the subheading 'Diary extracts'.

17 Add a right-aligned header to include your name and a date field. Insert page numbers at the bottom right-hand side of the page. Number the first page.

18 Print your work and save the document as: **Answer 1**. Apply the password 'Samuel' to protect your file. Close your file.

19 From the Task Files folder, open the file: **Table**. Change the text to Table, and Sort in order of colour.

20 Create a column chart from the table. Format the columns to the appropriate colour to correspond with the data. Right-align the chart.

21 Create a row at the bottom of the table and insert a formula that will calculate the amount of paper used each month. Save your work as: **Answer 2**. Print out the document. Close your file.

22 Mail Merge the file **Letter Form** with the file **Letter Data** to a New Document. Sort the data in order of surname. Produce letters to those living in Accrington. Print pages 3 and 4 on one A4 sheet. Save your work as: **Answer 3**.

Practice assignment answers

Answer 1

1669

Samuel Pepys

diary extracts

Contents

1

---

1 JAN

I found my Lord Sandwich, Peterburgh, and Sir Ch. Herberd; and presently after them come my Lord Hinchingbrooke, Mr Sidny, and Sir Wm. Godolphin; and after greeting them, and some time spent in talk, dinner was brought up, one dish after another, but a dish at a time; but all so good, but above all things, the variety of wines, and excellent of their kind, I had for them, and all in so good order, that they were mightily pleased, and myself full of content at it; and indeed it was, of a dinner of about six or eight dishes, as noble as any man-men need to have I think - at least, all was done in the noblest manner that ever I had any, and I have rarely seen in my life better anywhere else - even at the Court.

So to my wife's chamber, and there supped and got her cut my hair and look my shirt, for I have itched mightily these six or seven days; and when all came to all, she finds that I am lousy-lousy, having found in my head and body above 20 lice, little and great; which I wonder at, being more than I have had, I believe, almost these twenty years.

FEBRUARY 23RD

I now took them *[his wife and girl servants]* to Westminster Abbey and there did show them all the tombs very finely, having one with us alone ... and here we did see, by particular-particular favour, the body of Queen Katherine of Valois, and had her upper part of her body in my hands. And I did kiss her mouth, reflecting upon it that I did kiss a Queen, and that this was my birthday, 36 year old, that I did first kiss a Queen.

MARCH 1ST

But here I do hear first that my Lady Paulina Montagu did die yesterday; at which I went to my Lord's lodgings, but he is shut up with sorrow and so not to be spoken with .... *[Paulina was Sandwich's second daughter an died of "a consumption" in her 20th year]*

MARCH 6TH

This day my wife made it appear to me that my late entertainment this week cost me above 12l, an expense which I am almost ashamed of, though it is but once in a great while, and is the end for which in the most part we live, to have such a merry day once or twice in a man's life.

2

APRIL 8TH

Going this afternoon through Smithfield, I did see a coach run over the coachman's neck and stand upon it, and yet the man rose up and was well after it, which I thought a wonder.

April 13th ... as God would have it I spied Deb which made my heart and head to work; ... and I run after her and I observed she endeavoured to avoid me, but I did speak to her and she to me ... and so, with my heart full of surprise and disorder, I away ....

... so home to my wife ... But, God forgive me, I hardly know how to put on confidence enough to speak as innocent, having had this passage today with Deb, though only, God knows, by accident. But my great pain is lest God Almighty shall suffer me to find out this girl, whom indeed~~endeed~~ I love, and with a bad amour; but I will pray to God to give me grace to forbear it.

APRIL 26TH

I am told ... of a great fire happened~~happenned~~ in Durham-yard last night, burning the house of one - Hungerford, who was to come to town to it this night; an so the house is burned, new furnished, by carelessness~~carelesness~~ of the girl sent to take off a candle from a bunch of candles, which she did by burning it off, and left the rest, as it is supposed, on fire. The King and Court was here, it seems, and stopped the fire by blowing up of the next house.

APRIL 30TH

I did make the workmen drink, and saw my coach cleaned and oiled~~oyled~~; and staying among poor people there in the alley, did hear them call their fat child "punch" which pleased me mightily, that word being become a word of common use for all that is thick and short.

MAY 1ST

Up betimes, called up by my tailor, and there first put on a summer suit this year - but it was not my fine one of flowered tabby vest and coloured camelot~~camelott~~ tunic, because it was too fine with the gold lace at the hands, that I was afeared to be seen in it - but put on the stuff-suit I made the last year, which is now repaired; and so did go to the office in it and sat all the morning, the day looking as if it would be foul~~fowle~~.

At noon home to dinner, and there find my wife extraordinary~~extraorrdinary~~ fine with her flowered tabby gown that she made two years ago, now laced exceeding pretty, and indeed~~endeed~~ was fine all over - and mighty earnest to go, though the day was very lowering, and she would have me put on my fine suit, which I did; and so anon we went alone through the town with our new Liveries of serge, and the horses' manes and tails tied with red ribbon

3

and the standards thus gilt with varnish and all clean, and green reigns~~raynes~~, that people did mightily look upon us; and the truth is, I did not see any coach more pretty, or more gay, than ours all the day.

MAY 10TH

to my Lord Crewe ... A stranger, a country gentleman, was with him, and he pleased with my discourse accidentally about the decay of gentlemen's families in the country, telling us that the old rule was that a family might remain 50 miles from London 100 year, 100 mile off from London 200 years, and so, farther or nearer London, more or less years. He also told us that he hath heard his father say that in his time it was so rare for a country gentleman to come to London, that when he did come, he used to make his will before he set out.

Thence walked a little with Creed, who tells me he hears how fine my horses and coach are, and advises me to avoid being noted for it; which I was vexed to hear taken notice of, it being what I feared; and Povy told me of my gold-lace sleeves in the park yesterday, which vexed me also, so as to resolve never to appear in Court with it, but presently have it taken off, as it is fit I should.

MAY 16TH

I all the afternoon drawing up a foul draft of my petition to the Duke of York about my eyes, for leave to spend three or four months out of the office, drawing it so as to give occasion to a voyage abroad....

[It was presented on the 19th May, and refers~~referes~~ to the "ill condition whereto the restless exercises of his Eyes requisite to the seasonable dispatching of the Work~~Worke~~ of his Place during the late War~~Warr~~ have unhappily reduced him .. he has fruitlessly made many medicinal attempts ... but is told by his doctors that nothing but a considerable relaxation *from Work~~Worke~~ can be depended upon either for recovery of what Portion of his Sight he~~hee~~ hath lost, or securing the remainder"]

... And thus ends all that I doubt I shall ever be able to do with my own eyes in the keeping of my journal~~journall~~, I being not able to do it any longer, having done now so long as to undo my eyes almost every time that I take a pen in my hand; and therefore, whatever comes of it, I must forbear; and therefore resolve~~reolve~~ from this time forward to have it kept by my people in long-hand, and must therefore be contented to set down no more than it is fit for them and all the world to know; or if there be anything (which cannot be much, now my amours to Deb are past, and my eyes hindering me in almost all other pleasures), I must endeavour to keep a margin in my book open, to add here and there a note in

4

PEPYS' SHORTHAND 1

shorthand with my own hand. And so I betake myself to that course which is almost as much as to see myself go into my grave - for which, and all the discomforts that will accompany my being blind, the good God prepare me.

Completed the Exercise? <u>Yes</u>

5

Your name here   02/02/2003

D
Deb · 3,4
Duke · 4

G
God · 3,5

K
King · 3

L
Lord · 2,4

T
tailor · 3

W
wife · 2,3

6

Answer 2

PAPER USAGE (REAMS)

	JAN	FEB	MAR	APR	MAY	JUN
BLUE	25	21	27	35	21	19
GREEN	23	27	25	22	21	17
WHITE	40	32	20	15	14	35
YELLOW	12	13	9	2	8	9
	100	93	81	74	64	80

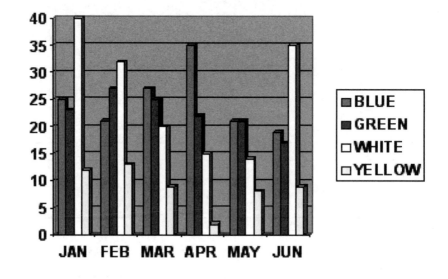

Answer 3

THE WORKS
21 Derby Street
NORTHWICH
Cheshire

Customer Service 01254 123456

02/02/2003

Mrs Heys
6 Quarry Street
ACCRINGTON
Lancs

Dear Mrs Heys

Thank you for your order and your deposit of £325.00. We will forward your receipt with the delivery date details.

In the meantime, if you have any further questions, please contact the Customer Service Centre on the above telephone number.

Yours sincerely

Julie Jones
Sales Advisor

THE WORKS
21 Derby Street
NORTHWICH
Cheshire

Customer Service 01254 123456

02/02/2003

Mr Nicholson
10 North Road
ACCRINGTON
Lancs

Dear Mr Nicholson

Thank you for your order and your deposit of £400.00. We will forward your receipt with the delivery date details.

In the meantime, if you have any further questions, please contact the Customer Service Centre on the above telephone number.

Yours sincerely

Julie Jones
Sales Advisor